Harmonic Materials
in
Tonal Music

A Programed Course

Part I

SEVENTH EDITION

Paul O. Harder

Greg A. Steinke
The University of Arizona

Allyn and Bacon
Boston   London   Toronto   Sydney   Tokyo   Singapore

Senior Series Editor: Steve Hull
Editorial Assistant: Brenda Conaway
Production Coordinator: Catherine Martin
Cover Administrator: Linda Dickinson
Manufacturing Buyer: Megan Cochran

Library of Congress Cataloging-in-Publication Data

Harder, Paul O.
    Harmonic materials in tonal music : a programed course / Paul O.
  Harder, Greg A. Steinke. -- 7th ed.
      p.   cm.
    Includes bibliographical references and indexes.
    ISBN 0-205-15802-1 (v. 1). -- ISBN 0-205-15804-8 (v. 2)
    1. Harmony--Programmed instruction.   I. Steinke, Greg A., 1942-
  . II. Title.
  MT50.H26   1993
  781.2'5'077--dc20
                                                    93-30223
                                                        CIP
                                                        MN

Printed in the United States of America

10 9 8 7 6 5 4 3 2 1   97 96 95 94 93

Contents

1.0

2.0

3.0

4.0

5.0

6.0

7.0

8.0

9.0

Preface to the Seventh Edition

It is a challenging task to revise a book which has already enjoyed many years of success and had been through five editions over more than twenty years. It was indeed an honor also to have been asked to undertake the revision of the sixth edition, and it was with some trepidation that I approached the task. However, I have had a deep belief in these books ever since I first used them as a very young theory teacher back in 1967 when they were first available. With a lot of history behind me, the highest respect and regard for all of Paul Harder's diligent efforts over the years on these books, I offered various revisions and enhancements to the books which I believe keep to the original spirit of Dr. Harder's programed concept, and which I hope all users have found helpful as they worked through these pages.

In making the revisions, I tried to respond to comments which were made available to me from Dr. Harder's estate, reviewers and current users of the books. The revisions were most apparent in additions made to the supplementary exercises, and some additions to the appendix material. In selected places throughout the book I tried to clarify definitions or to demonstrate to the reader there are always alternatives to those ideas presented in the book, and that the reader should explore them on his/her own or in class with one's instructor. In making those changes, I hoped that the differences in theoretical and analytical approaches (which I know will always be there) would work comfortably with these books and also provide many interesting points of discussion in class. I was quite sure that Dr. Harder never intended the volume to be the final definitive answer, but rather to provide an informed point of departure to explore the many anomalies that are always to be found in musics everywhere.

In the current edition further refinements have been made to individual frames, supplementary exercises and the appendix materials. The recordings which have accompanied the last several editions have been redone in a more contemporary form (both sound and venues — cassettes and CD). Some adjustments have been made to the book layout and type fonts, which should also help in using the book. A full instructor's manual in now available.

The exposition of the material is presented via a step by step process, which, to some, may seem mechanical, but it does ensure, in general, a good understanding of the basic tenets of the harmonic materials of the so-called common practice period in music. I would emphasize that this approach does not preclude presenting alternatives nor the exploration of other possibilities of how composers may work with various cause and effect relationships as they write rather than following any set of "rules". A very rich learning experience can be created for all concerned, instructor as well as student, by exploring together all the many exceptions to the so-called "rules" or principles. In so doing, it becomes possible to link all that is studied to actual musical literature or to create many varieties of assignments to solidify the understanding of the basic harmonic framework presented within these pages.

I am still very grateful both to Mildred Harder who recommended me to undertake these revisions and to Allyn and Bacon for accepting that recommendation and providing helpful comments and support throughout the revision process. I also wish to thank Mrs. Harder for providing me access to all notes and support materials Dr. Harder used in the original creation of these books and for her ever helpful comments and moral support to complete this project. I would also thank colleagues Drs. David Stech, Dr. Larry Solomon, Dr. J. Timothy Kolosick, Dr. Timothy Kloth, Dr. Kenneth Rummery, Dr. Margaret Mayer, Dr. Deborah Kavasch and Dr. Lewis Strouse for their comments, encouragement and assistance on revision ideas. I am grateful to all concerned and am most appreciative of the help they have all provided. And finally, special thanks go to my wife, Kari (who assisted with the bulk of the computer inputing for this current edition), and my two boys, Carl and Kyle, for being patient and quiet while I have worked and always offering moral support as well as helpful comments. I hope users of this volume will find many hours of rich, musical learning to enhance their developing musicianship.

GAS

Preface to the Earlier Fifth Edition

The refinements incorporated into the fifth edition are designed to make this book an even more useful aid for learning the materials and practices of tonal harmony. One change concerns the summaries that follow the expository section of each chapter: many have been expanded for a more complete overview of the main points covered. The summaries, plus all new mastery frames, help the learner assess or comprehend the material in each chapter before proceeding to the next. Another change involves the supplementary assignments, which are also all new. In addition, they are now organized so each may be removed from the book as a separate entity, facilitating their submission to the instructor for evaluation.

The chief emphasis in this two-part study of tonal harmony is on the basic elements of harmony that have retained their validity throughout the period from about 1600 to 1900. Music from this period is still very much a part of our musical life. Not only does a large part of the current repertoire consist of eighteenth- and nineteteenth-century music, but tonal harmony is the basis of practically all commercial music. All composers, no matter what style they generally may employ, turn to tonal harmony when such material is appropriate to their expressive purpose. This book is not devoted to the study of any one composer's works, nor is it limited to four-part writing; various applications of harmonic principles are shown in musical examples drawn from a variety of periods and compositional types.

Since most of the music we hear and perform is based on tonal harmony, it is essential that serious students become familiar with this system. For the composer, competence in writing requires thorough understanding of techniques practiced by composers of previous generations. For the performer, the ability to convey delicate nuances and subtleties of phrasing often stems from a cultivated sensitivity to harmonic processes.

Experience has shown that the type of programed instruction used in this book can lead to rapid, yet thorough mastery of musical concepts and techniques. Also, it has proved to versatile in that it can be used not only by a single student working independently, but also by students in large classes. Still more important is the flexibility that programed material brings to the instructor. the core of knowledge contained in this book may be expanded by emphasis upon creative writing, analysis, or the study of music literature. Because students evaluate their own exercises, the instructor is free to prepare more vital and creative supplementary learning experiences.

the development of this course was supported by the Educational Development Program at Michigan State University. The author is grateful to Dr. John Dietrich, Assistant Provost, and Dr. Robert Davis, Director of the Educational Development Program, for their assistance; also to Drs. Jere Hutcheson, Clifford Pfeil, and Gary White, who helped develop practical classroom methods. Particular tribute, though, must be paid to the many students who, over a period of several years, assisted in proving out the approaches incorporated in this book. Thanks also go to Rita Fuszek, Professor of Music at California State University, Fullerton, the diligent pianist who recorded the examples contained in the cassettes that accompany this book. And finally, special thanks go to my wife, Mildred, who has not only typed countless pages over the years, but provided helpful comment and moral support.

Paul O. Harder
(1923–1986)

How to Use This Book

This book features the use of programed instruction to convey conceptual information and provide drills to develop techniques for handling harmonic materials. In programmed instruction, information is presented in small, carefully sequenced parcels which combine in cumulative fashion to give students mastery of the subject. The parcels into which the material is divided are called *frames*. Most frames require a written response, which may be a word ot two, or consist of the solution of a musical problem. Since correct answers are provided by the book itself, this type of material is self-correcting; thus students may work entirely alone and proceed at their own pace. When used in class, supplemeentary examples and lessons may be supplied by the instructor as he or she sees fit. (Please note that the answers to the supplementary assignments are contained in the instructor's manual, available on request from the publisher.)

The principal part of each frame is located on the right-hand side of the page. The answers, which appear on the left-hand side, should be covered with a slip of paper or a ruler (merely the hand will do). After the response is written, the appropriate answer is uncovered so the response may be checked immediately. Since each step in this process is small, few mistakes are made. Because of this, learning is reinforced and misconceptions have little chance to become part of the student's thinking.

To the Student

Do not begin this study of tonal harmony without thorough knowledge and/or review of the fundamentals of music including scales, key signatures, intervals, and triads. You are strongly urged to review the author's *Basic Materials in Music Theory*, also published by Allyn and Bacon.

This book features the use of programed instruction to convey conceptual information and provide drills to develop techniques for handling harmonic materials. In programed instruction, information is presented in small carefully sequenced parcels that combine in cumulative fashion to help you master the subject. The parcels into which the material is divided are called *frames*. Most frames require a written response, which may be a word or two, or perhaps the solution to a musical problem.

The principal part of each frame is located on the right-hand side of the page. The answers, which appear on the left-hand side, should be covered with a slip of paper or a ruler (merely the hand will do). After you write your response, uncover the answer and check your work immediately. There are many cases in which your answer need not be exactly the same as that supplied by the text. You should consider your response correct if it conveys the same meaning as the one given. Use common sense to decide whether or not you comprehend a particular item. Because each step is small, you should make few mistakes.

Each chapter ends with a series of "mastery" frames. These frames allow you to evaluate your mastery of key points — concepts and skills essential to coping with matters that lie ahead. *Do not proceed unless you handling of the mastery frames assures you that you are ready to continue.*

Mastery frames are identified with double numbers to prevent confusion with the frames that constitute the body of the text. References to the frames that cover the subject of each question are provided along with the correct answers. Avail yourself to these references in order to focus remedial study precisely upon the points missed.

Many musical examples are given in the text to acquaint you with the way various composers use harmonic devices. You should play these at the piano, or program them in a computer for playback, so that they are actually *heard*. It is not sufficient to approach this study on an intellectual level alone; you must have command of the harmonic vocabulary as an aural phenomenon as well. The prupose of cenceptualizing musical processes is to render more understandable the responses elicited by the auditory stimuli of music. Remember, music is an *aural* art; it apprehended better by the ear than by the eye.

A ■ beside a frame indicates that the music in that frame is reproduced on the cassette or compact disc.

An Important Perspective for the Study of Harmony

One would suppose that, by now, the study of tonal harmony would be passé. After all, traditional harmonic tonality, with its wide, attendant vocabulary of chords, has become more diffused and of a broader scope through the compositions of the impressionists of the late nineteenth century and the atonalists of the early twentieth century. The impressionists — Debussy in particular — created an expression of the conception of tonality through the use of non-tertian chords and nonfunctional streams of chords, as well as by the expansion of tonal frontiers. By the end of the first decade of the twentieth century, Arnold Schönberg had shown in works such as *Pierrot Lunaire* that expressive music could indeed be created without resorting to either traditional tonality or tertain harmony. The dodecaphonic, or twelve-tone, system was designed to effectively negate any lingering influences of traditional harmonic practices. This system, as employed by members of the second Viennese School (Webern and Berg, in addition to Schönberg), as well as by countless others during the succeeding decades, led to a larger body of music, including many highly expressive works.

Harmonic music, however, is still with us. Far from being dead, it is alive and well. Most of the music heard through mass media, and practically all commercial music, is based on traditional harmonic practices. This is true, also, of music performed in churches and studied in schools. Even concert and recital programs reveal a stubborn adherence to the standard repertoire, with the inclusion of only an occasional nontonal work. There is, of course, the all-too-rare program devoted exclusively to advanced music. Unfortunately such programs have little impact, considering the overwhelming amount of more traditional music heard.

What accounts for the persistence of traditional music? Reasons can only be stated as speculation. A few follow:

1. There are those who would point to the "natural" basis of harmonic music. Because the natural harmonic series is a phenomenon of nature, the generation of chords by thirds and the relation of roots to the tonic according to percepts derived from the series can be seen not only as being ordained by nature, but also as possessing special moral sanction.

2. Perhaps because most people in our society, from birth, have heard little other than harmonic music, preference is given to the familiar; choice is made on the basis of conditioning, which produces an inertia of values.

3. Music in which tones bear relatively simple acoustical relations to one another is easier both to sing and to apprehend. Much folk music, for example, displays preference for limited range and relatively small intervals, as well as emphasis on the perfect fourth and fifth-intervals which have special tonal significance.

4. It is apparent that the expressive resources of tonal music have not been exhausted. The rapidly changing styles of commercial music demonstrate that fresh draughts of musical expression still remain to be drawn from the well of harmonic resources.

Rationale aside, harmonic music clearly constitutes the bulk of what is heard by our society at large. It also dominates the music studied and performed by students in our schools of music. These realities justify the continued study of tonal harmony, and the time is not in sight when this study will be without meaning and thus disppear from the standard music curriculum.

The two basic parameters of music are *temporal (time)* and *sonic* (sound). With respect to the sonic parameter, two principal methods of organization have evolved in Western music: *counterpoint* (linear) and *harmony* (chordal). The technique of counterpoint developed much earlier than the concept of harmony as an independant musical principle. From about the beginning of the tenth century to nearly 1600, the chief organizing principles were related to counterpoint. But from the beginning, the effect of voices sounding together was recognized as an important factor. This is evidenced by the changing preferences for intervals during the course of musical evolution.

Early in the development of counterpoint, the chief consonances were: perfect unisons, octaves, fourths, and fifths. Open sonorities such as 1-5-8 were the main consonant sonorities, with complete triads (1-3-5) appearing as passing occurrences. The frequency of triads gradually increased after 1300, occurring even at cadence points, except for the final cadence where perfect consonances (1-5-8) were still preferred. From about the middle of the fifteenth century, complete triads in both root position and first inversion predominated, but music from this period displays no systematic approach to harmonic progression, except at the cadences, where plagal, authentic, and Phrygian cadences are used.

After 1600, the preeminence of the first, fourth, and fifth scale degrees began to be established, and greater consistency of root movement developed. This led to the establishment of major/minor tonality, which supplanted the modal system of the medieval and Renaissance periods. During the Baroque period, the vocabulary of chords was enlarged to include various altered chords such as the Neapolitan sixth and secondary dominants. Chromaticism and systematic modulation also developed at this time. In response to the classical ideals of clarity, lightness and balance, harmonic action tended to be simpler and more formula driven. The form-defining function of contrasting tonalities, however, became even more important, also, there was more frequent modulation to distant keys.

Harmony received its fullest development during the romantic period (1825-1900), during which time the tonal horizon was pushed back to the very limits of equal temperament, and the repertoire of chords was expanded by the use of the complete chromatic scale. Frequent use of altered chords, coupled with modulations to distant keys, led to the eventual disintegration of tonality, and the fall of tonality brought down the whole structure of tonal relations and chord structures associated with tertain harmony. But, as we have seen, harmonic music refuses to die; its emotive power is still stong. And, although it appears that the evolution of harmony was complete by 1900, harmonic materials may still be exploited for new ends.

The evolution of harmony may also be traced through the writings of various theorists. For this purpose we shall review briefly some of the major contributions to the field of harmonic theory. It is surprising that recognition of harmony as an independant musical parameter occurred so late. After all, several contrapuntal lines produce simultaneous sounds, and for several centuries prior to 1600, many of these sounds resulted in chords. But pre-baroque technique exploited the interval as the basic constructive unit — the concept of chord did not exist. What we recognize as chords were viewed then as conglomerations of intervals. The first recognition of the chord as an entity occurred in Gioseffo Zarlino's *Istituzioni armoniche* of 1558. In this work Zarlino refers to the *harmonia perfetta*, which results from the first six tones of the natural harmonic series. It is, in effect, the major triad. Being the first to recognize the triad as a harmonic entity, Zarlino is the father of modern harmonic theory.

A still greater contribution to harmonic theory was made by Jean-Philippe Rameau, whose treatise *Traité de l'Harmonie* was published in 1722. Many of the principles set fourth by Rameau are still employed today to explain harmonic processes. Rameau's writings are extensive and involved. His chief contributions, however, are threefold:

1. He postulated that the lowest note of the triad in 1-3-5 position is the root and is the generator of the 3rd and 5th. Also, this note (1) remains the root when the chord is inverted to either 3-5-8 (first inversion) or 5-8-10 (second inversion).

2. The roots of chords, as opposed to the actual bass line, constitute the "fundamental," and the fundamental bass is the true motivator of the harmony. The result of this principle is to reduce the number of harmonic entities and provide a simple method for relating chords to one another and to the tonal center.

3. The symmetrical structure of harmonic tonality was identified by Rameau, who, recognizing the fundamental accoustical nature of the perfect fifth, also saw the subdominant and dominant as straddling the tonic (IV-I-V), the dominant a fifth higher, the subdominant a fifth lower. It was Rameau who first used the term *sous-dominante* to designate the "lower" dominant.

Rameau, like Zarlino, based his theories on the natural harmonic series and mathematics. Most later harmonic theorists did likewise. Some, however, chose other bases for their speculations. For example, in 1754 Guiseppe Tartini published his treatise *Trattato di musica,* in which reference is made not only to the natural harmonic series and mathematics, but also to geometry. In 1853, Moritz Hauptmann published his *Die Natur der Harmonik und Metrik*, in which a philosophical approach based on Hegel's dialectical metaphysics is employed.

The theorists reviewed here, plus many others, * felt that they were dealing with harmony as a science, that basic principles which would explain music phenomena, and more, lay hidden, waiting only to be discovered and proved. But this has proved to be a chimera; for no harmonic theory, including Rameau's is free of inner contradictions. There have been many near misses; but nature has not cooperated by providing a closed system to tone relations, at least in terms of the kind of music with which people have to date been concerned.

---

*Please see the Bibliography for Further Study for sources on other theorists.

Chapter 1.0
Some Definitions

The elements of music include rhythm, melody, timbre, texture, and harmony. Some of these are virtually universal; they are exploited in music of all ages and cultures. Music without rhythm, for example, can hardly be imagined. Harmony, on the other hand, is missing from much primitive and oriental music. Even in Western music harmony was established as an independent element in the relatively recent past. From only about 1600 did consistent usage gradually establish patterns of harmonic and tonal relations, which eventually were codified by theorists to form a "science of harmony." But harmony quickly became a central concern, and ultimately superceded even counterpoint, which had provided the technical basis for musical composition since about the ninth century.

During the eighteenth and nineteenth centuries composers were so preoccupied with the expanding harmonic system that other musical elements — particularly rhythm — were neglected. But harmony served these composers well. It provided the fountainhead of style and expression — from harmony stemmed not only melody, but form. Most of the music heard today (this includes nearly all commercial music) is either from the eighteenth or nineteenth centuries, or is based on similar harmonic principles. For this reason the study of harmony is essential for those who wish to be knowledgeable listeners or competent performers.

Harmony has two dimensions. One is "vertical" — several tones sounding simultaneously (chords); the other is "horizontal" — successions of chords within a tonal system. Thus the study of harmony involves two things: types of chords; and how chords relate to one another. We shall begin by explaining what is meant by tonal music. Next, several terms which relate to tonality and chords will be defined and some basic analytical symbols will also be introduced.

	1.1 Most of the music composed between 1600 and 1900 is based upon major and minor scales. Music of this type is generally called TONAL music. In tonal music one tone (the keynote) predominates over the other tones of the scale. The keynote is the same as the first note of the scale. Music in which one tone generally predominates over
tonal	the other tones of the scale is called _____ music.
B-flat	1.2 What is the keynote of the B-flat major scale? _____
E	1.3 What is the keynote of the E minor scale? _____
	1.4 Music which is based upon the C major scale is said to be in the key of C major. The KEY of a composition corresponds to the key-note of the scale which is used.

F-sharp

A composition in the key of F-sharp minor is based

primarily upon the _____minor scale.

1.5   But being "in a key" involves more than merely using the notes of a particular scale. The melody below, for example, uses some of the notes of the G major scale, and the prominence of the keynote (G) is heightened because the melody begins and ends on G.

Carey, *America*

Only five notes of the G major scale are used. Count the number of times each note occurs and list them below:

F♯	2
G	6
A	4
B	3
C	1

F♯	_____
G	_____
A	_____
B	_____
C	_____

---

keynote (or tonic)

1.6   Iteration (repetition) is an important means of causing one tone to predominate over other tones. In simple tonal music the tone which receives the greatest stress

through iteration is often the _____.

---

tonality

1.7   It is common to speak of music as being in a particular key. This is a way of identifying the scale which serves as the basis for the music. The term TONALITY means practically the same thing as *key*. This term is often used in a broader sense, however, to refer to any music which centers on a single tone regardless of the tonal system employed. Within the context of this study the terms *key* and *tonality* will be used synonymously.

A composition in the key of C major may also be said

to be in the _____ of C major.

A major.

1.8   What is the tonality of a composition which is based

primarily upon the A major scale? _____

key	1.9 Music in which a single tone tends to predominate over the others may be said to be TONAL. In tonal music one tone takes precedence over all the others; this tone is called the TONAL CENTER. What is another name for the tonal center ? The _____ center.
first	1.10 The keynote is which note of the scale? The _____.
Yes.	1.11 Do the terms tonal center, key center, and keynote have ap proximately the same meaning? _____

(No response.)	1.12 The points made thus far are these:
	    The *key* of a composition may be established by using the notes of a particular scale; by beginning and ending on the keynote; and by iteration of the keynote.
	    The *tonal center* is that tone which predominates over all the others. This tone is also called the *keynote*.
	    Any music which tends to be oriented to a tonal center is said to be *tonal*. The *tonality* of a composition corresponds to the tonal center.

tonal	1.13 Harmony which is associated with tonal music is called TONAL HARMONY. Within the limits of this study tonal harmony will mean harmony based upon major and minor scales. Harmony based upon the major-minor scale system is called _____ harmony.
tones	1.14 Before continuing with the study of tonal harmony we must make some important distinctions. In the next few frames we shall note the difference between *intervals, chords,* and *triads.* The basic component of harmony is the chord. These, in turn, are the result of several tones sounding simultaneously. Chords are vertical structures consisting of several_____
	1.15 The simultaneous sounding of two tones produces a *harmonic interval,* but do not confuse an interval with a chord. Although a single interval may occasionally imply a chord, *at least three tones are required to* produce a complete chord.* --- *In impressionistic music as well as some later twentieth century styles, two tones do occasionally function as a chord. In such cases the term *dyad* may be used.

chords	Vertical structures form either intervals or _____.
three	1.16 Two tones sounding together produce an interval. A chord, however, consists of at least _____ tones.
Yes.	1.17 Are all of the structures below chords? _____
No. *(Item (3) contains only two notes.* *This is called an interval.)*	1.18 Are all of the structures below chords? _____
Yes.	1.19 A chord of three tones is also called a TRIAD. Are all of the chords below triads? _____
	1.20 Although any three tones sounding simultaneously produce a triad, within the system of tonal harmony triads are constructed of superimposed thirds.

The note on which a triad is built is called the ROOT. Triads consisting of superimposed thirds are part of the

tonal

system of _____ harmony.

1.21   Consider each note of the C major scale below to be the root of a triad. Write a triad on each note. (*Use no accidentals.*)

KEY OF C MAJOR

1.22   The triads you have just written use only the notes of the C major scale. These are called DIATONIC triads. Diatonic triads are constructed only of notes contained in the scale being used.
      Triads which utilize only the notes of the scale are

diatonic

called_____ triads.

---

(3).
(*E-flat is not a diatonic tone in the key of G major.*)

1.23   Which of the triads below is NOT a diatonic triad?

_____.

(Key of G major)

---

(1).
(*B-natural is not a diatonic tone in the key of B-flat major.*)

1.24   Which of the triads below is NOT a diatonic triad?

_____.

(Key of B♭ major)

No.

1.25   If a triad contains a tone which is foreign to the key,

can it be called diatonic?_____

1.26　A triad may be constructed on each of the seven degrees of the major scale.

KEY OF D MAJOR

Is each of these triads a diatonic triad?_____

Yes.

1.27 How many diatonic triads are contained in a

major key? _____

Seven.

1.28　Construct a diatonic triad on each degree of the E-flat major scale.

1.29　Construct a diatonic triad on each degree of the B major scale.

1.30　Diatonic triads utilize only the notes which are included in the scale being used. In the *harmonic* minor scale the raised seventh degree is considered diatonic since it is part of the scale. The seven diatonic triads in the key of D minor, using the harmonic minor scale, are shown below.

Yes.
(C-sharp is a diatonic note in the D harmonic minor scale.)

Some of the triads above contain an accidental (C- sharp).

Are these diatonic triads? _____

1.31   Construct a diatonic triad on each degree of the E harmonic minor scale. *(Apply accidentals where necessary.)*

1.32   Construct a diatonic triad on each degree of the F harmonic minor scale. *(Apply accidentals where necessary.)*

(No response.)

1.33   *Intervals* combine to produce the basic component of harmony — chords. *Triads* are chords of three tones. In the system of tonal harmony triad tones are related by thirds. *Diatonic* triads use only scale tones.

1.34   Chord symbols consisting of Roman numerals are used to identify triads built on the various degrees of the scale.*

KEY OF D MAJOR

I   ii   iii   IV   V   vi   vii°

KEY OF D MINOR

i   ii°   III⁺   iv   V   VI   vii°

---

*Composers in the common-practice period do not necessarily confine their selection of diatonic triads in minor to the harmonic form of the minor scale. In the minor mode some prefer the major quality mediant triad (III) rather than the augmented form (III⁺) derived from the harmonic minor. In analysis, one should be alert for these varying occurences.

scale	The Roman numerals used to identify the various triads of a key correspond to the degrees of the_____.
major	1.35 Notice in the preceding frame that the Roman numerals have different forms depending upon the quality of the triads. *Study the chart below:* TYPE OF TRIAD SYMBOL Major = I, IV, V, (III) Minor = ii, iii, vi Diminished = ii°, vii° Augmented = III$^+$ A Roman numeral consisting of capital letters denotes a _____triad.
plus *(or cross)*	1.36 An augmented triad is indicated by a large Roman numeral followed by a _____sign.
circle	1.37 A diminished triad is indicated by a *small* Roman numeral followed by a _____.
True.	1.38 A minor triad is indicated by a *small* Roman numeral. (True/False)_____.
Major Diminished Augmented Minor	1.39 Name the triad *quality* (major, minor, diminished, or augmented) indicated by each chord symbol. (1) IV _____ (2) ii° _____ (3) III$^+$ _____ (4) vi _____
No. *(Item (3) represents a diminished triad.)*	1.40 Do all of the Roman numerals below represent triads of identical quality? _____. (1) vi (2) iii (3) ii° (4) iv
Yes	1.41 Do all of the Roman numerals below represent triads of identical quality? _____. (1) I (2) VI (3) IV (4) V

Major	1.42 What type of triad is indicated by the Roman numerals in the preceding frame? _____
(3).	1.43 Which Roman numeral represents a *minor* triad?_____ (1) V (2) III⁺ (3) ii (4) vii°
(4).	1.44 Which Roman numeral represents an *augmented* triad? _____ (1) ii° (2) III (3) vi (4) III⁺
(2).	1.45 Which Roman numersl represents a *diminished* triad? _____ (1) ii (2) vii° (3) III (4) V
(3).	1.46 Which Roman numeral represents a major triad? _____ (1) III⁺ (2) ii (3) IV (4) iv
 I ii iii IV V vi vii°	1.47 Write the remaining Roman numerals to represent the triads built on the seven degrees of the E-flat major scale. *(Be sure the quality of each triad is reflected by the form of the Roman numeral.)* I __ __ __ __ __ __
 i ii° III⁺ iv V VI vii°	1.48 Write the Roman numeral to represent the triad built on the seven degrees of the E-flat harmonic minor scale. *(Be sure the quality of each triad is reflected by the form of the Roman numeral.)* __ __ __ __ __ __ __

	1.49 Complete the list below: THE QUALITY OF TRIADS USING THE MAJOR SCALE
1st: major	The triad on the 1st degree is _____.
2nd: minor	The triad on the 2nd degree is_____.
3rd: minor	The triad on the 3rd degree is_____.
4th: major	The triad on the 4th degree is _____.
5th: major	The triad on the 5th degree is_____.
6th: minor	The triad on the 6th degree is_____.
7th: diminished	The triad on the 7th degree is_____.
	1.50 Complete the list below: THE QUALITY OF TRIADS USING THE HARMONIC MINOR SCALE
1st: minor	The triad on the 1st degree is_____.
2nd: diminished	The triad on the 2nd degree is_____.
3rd: augmented	The triad on the 3rd degree is_____ .
4th: minor	The triad on the 4th degree is_____.
5th: major	The triad on the 5th degree is_____.
6th: major	The triad on the 6th degree is_____.
7th: diminished	The triad on the 7th degree is _____.
minor	1.51 The quality of the triad on the fourth degree of the harmonic minor scale is_____.
major	1.52 The quality of the triad on the sixth degree of the harmonic minor scale is_____.
minor	1.53 The quality of the triad on the first degree of the harmonic minor scale is_____.
major	1.54 The quality of the triad on the fifth degree of the harmonic minor scale is_____.
False. *(This triad is minor.)*	1.55 The triad on the sixth degree of the major scale is major. (True/False)_____.

True.	1.56 The triad on the second degree of the harmonic minor scale is diminished. (True/False) _____
False. *(This triad is augmented.)*	1.57 The triad on the third degree of the harmonic minor scale is major. (True/ False)_____.
I ii iii IV V vi vii°	1.58 Analyze with Roman numerals the triad built on the seven degrees of the G major scale. ___ ___ ___ ___ ___ ___ ___
i ii° III⁺ iv V VI vii°	1.59 Analyze with Roman numerals the triads built on the seven degrees of the G harmonic minor scale. ___ ___ ___ ___ ___ ___ ___
(No response.)	1.60 The benefit gained from using various forms of Roman numerals is that you are thereby made aware of the *specific quality* of each chord. This, in turn, increases your sensitivity to the actual sounds represented by the notes.
major	1.61 When analyzing with Roman numerals the key is identified by an abbreviation of its name followed by a colon (:). Compare the designations below: *E-flat major* = E♭: *E-flat minor* = e♭: Notice that a *capital* letter is used to indicate a major key, whereas a *lower case* letter is used for a minor key. The symbol (B:) represents the key of B_____.
(1) F: (2) a♭: (3) E:	1.62 Write the proper designation for each key. (1) F major _____ (2) A-flat minor _____ (3) E major _____

1.63 Write the proper designation for each key.

(1) g♯:
(1) G-sharp minor _____

(2) D:
(2) D major _____

(3) b♭:
(3) B-flat minor _____

1.64 What key is indicated by each symbol?

(1) A Major
(1) A: The key of _____

(2) C-sharp minor.
(2) c♯:   The key of _____

(3) D minor.
(3) d: The key of _____

1.65 What key is indicated by each symbol?

(1) B minor.
(1) b: The key of _____

(2) G-flat major.
(2) G♭:   The key of _____

(3) C-sharp major.
(3) C♯: The key of _____

1.66 Write the proper chord symbol in each case. *(Be sure to check the quality of each triad.)*

(1)   (2)   (3)
I   III⁺   ii

(1)   (2)   (3)

Bb: ___   e: ___   D: ___

1.67 Continue as in the preceding frame.

(1)   (2)   (3)
iv   iii   V

(1)   (2)   (3)

d: ___   Eb: ___   f♯: ___

1.68 Continue as in the preceding frame. *(Note use of bass clef.)*

(1)   (2)   (3)
IV   VI   V

(1)   (2)   (3)

Ab: ___   c♯: ___   Bb: ___

1.69   Continue as in the preceding frame.

(1)   (2)   (3)

g: ____   B: ____   bb: ____

(1)   (2)   (3)

vii°   vi   i

1.70   Write the triads indicated by the Roman numerals. *(No key signature is supplied, so you must apply accidentals to those notes which need them.)*

(1)   (2)   (3)

d: iv   A: V   Eb: iii

(1)   (2)   (3)

d: iv   A: V   Eb: iii

1.71   Continue as in the preceding frame.

(1)   (2)   (3)

g: vii°   c: VI   F#:   ii

(1)   (2)   (3)

g: vii°   c: VI   F#: ii

1.72   Continue as in the preceding frame.

(1)   (2)   (3)

Ab: vii°   c#:   V   a: III⁺

(1)   (2)   (3)

Ab: vii°   c#: V   a: III⁺

1.73   Continue as in the preceding frame.

(No response.)

1.74   The first step in harmonic analysis is to identify the key. This involves not only locating the tonal center, but also identifying the mode (major or minor). A capital letter represents a major key (A: = A major); a lower case letter represents a minor key (a: = A minor).

Active awareness of key and mode is absolutely essential to a knowledgeable approach to both performance and theoretical study. The symbols which have been introduced are designed to sharpen your perception and awareness.

Summary

In tonal music a single tone is caused to predominate over the others. This tone is called the *tonal center* and is the same as the *keynote* of the scale being used.

Two superimposed intervals of a third produce a chord of three tones called a *triad*. There are four types of triads in the major-minor scale system (major, minor, diminished and augmented). These four types of triads provide the basic harmonic material of tonal music.

For the purpose of analysis triads are identified by chord symbols consisting of Roman numerals. These correspond to the scale degrees on which the triads are built. Various forms of chord symbols are used to show the quality of each triad as below:

TRIAD QUALITY	SYMBOLS	
Major	I, IV, V, (III)	(capital letters)
Minor	ii, iii, vi	(lower case letters)
Diminished	ii°, vii°	(circle added to lower case letters)
Augmented	III+	(plus sign added to capital letters)

The terms that are explained in this chapter are listed below in chronological order:

tonal	tonal center	harmonic interval
keynote	tonal harmony	root
key	intervals	diatonic (triads)
iteration	chords	chord symbols
tonality	triads	Roman numerals

Mastery Frames

3. Tonal center. (1.1–.12)	1–1 Indicate the term on the right that conveys practically the same meaning as the one on the left. Keynote_____ 1. Tonality 2. Root 3. Tonal center
2. Key (1.4–.13)	1–2 Indicate the term on the right that conveys practically the same meaning as the one on the left. Tonality_____ 1. Chord 2. Key 3. Tonal harmony
(1) Interval (3) Chord (2) Chord (4) Interval (1.14–.19)	1–3 Identify each example as either an interval or a chord. (1)_____ (3)_____ (2)_____ (4)_____
3. (1.19)	1–4 How many tones are required to produce a triad?_____.
thirds (1.20)	1–5 Triads within the system of tonal harmony are based on a note called the *root*, and they are constructed of superimposed_____.

diatonic (1.22–.33)	1–6 Triads that employ only the notes of the prevailing key are called_____triads.
(2), (3). (1.22–.33)	1–7 Which are diatonic triads in the key of B-flat major?_____ (1) (2) (3) (4)
(1) Major (3) Diminished (2) Minor (4) Augmented (1.35–.46)	1–8 Identify the triad *quality* indicated by each of the chord symbols. (1) IV_____ (3) ii° _____ (2) vi _____ (4) III⁺ _____
(1) B-flat major (2) E major (3) F-sharp minor (4) G minor (1.61–.65)	1–9 Identify the key indicated by each of the symbols below. (1) B♭: _____ (2) E: _____ (3) f♯: _____ (4) g: _____
D: I ii iii IV V vi vii° (1.58)	1–10 Write chord symbols for each of the triads below. D: __ __ __ __ __ __ __
c: i ii° III⁺ iv V VI vii° (1.59)	1–11 Write chord symbols for each of the triads below. c: __ __ __ __ __ __ __

1–12   Indicate the type of triad that occurs on each degree of the *major* scale.

	Scale Degrees	Triad Types
(1) Major	(1)	_____
(2) Minor	(2)	_____
(3) Minor	(3)	_____
(4) Major	(4)	_____
(5) Major	(5)	_____
(6) Minor	(6)	_____
(7) Diminished	(7)	_____

(1.49)

1–13   Indicate the type of triad that occurs on each degree of the *harmonic minor* scale.

	Scale degrees	Triad Types
(1) Minor	(1)	_____
(2) Diminished	(2)	_____
(3) Augmented	(3)	_____
(4) Minor	(4)	_____
(5) Major	(5)	_____
(6) Major	(6)	_____
(7) Diminished	(7)	_____

(1.50)

Supplementary Assignments

The material supplied here is intended to be both useful in itself and suggestive of other supplementary work designed by instructors to serve their students' particular needs.

ASSIGNMENT 1–1   Name _____

1. Write a brief definition of each term.

    a. Keynote_____

    _____

    b. Tonality_____

    _____

    c. Tonal harmony_____

    _____

2. What note is the tonal center of the melody below?_____

3. Write a brief justification for your answer to question 2. _____

    _____

    _____

4. Write a single line melody that clearly establishes the key of B-flat major.

5. Identify the specific features of your melody that contribute to the establishment of the tonality.

    _____

6. Distinguish between "interval" and "chord." _____

    _____

    _____

7. What is a triad? _____

    _____

    _____

8. What is meant by the term "diatonic triad"? _____

    _____

    _____

9. Identify each example as either an interval or a chord.

    (1) _____   (4) _____

    (2) _____   (5) _____

    (3) _____   (6) _____

10. List the examples in the preceding question that are triads. _____

11. What intervals is the basic building block of triads in the tonal harmonic system? _____

12. Write all of the diatonic triads in the key of E major.

13. Write all of the diatonic triads in the key of G minor (harmonic form).

ASSIGNMENT 1–2

1.   List the *quality* of the diatonic triad on each degree of a major scale.

   Scale degree

   (1) _____   (5) _____

   (2) _____   (6) _____

   (3) _____   (7) _____

   (4) _____

2.   List the *quality* of the diatonic triad on each degree of a minor scale (harmonic form).

   (1) _____   (5) _____

   (2) _____   (6) _____

   (3) _____   (7) _____

   (4) _____

3.   Write the chord indicated by each chord symbol. (*Provide the necessary accidentals.*)

4.   Write the chord symbol for each chord.

5.   Write the chord symbol for each chord.

6.   Write the chord indicated by each chord symbol.

7. Which chord matches the chord symbol? _____

D: vii°

8. Which chord matches the chord symbol? _____

c: VI

9. Which chord matches the chord symbol? _____

a: III⁺

10. Which chord matches the chord symbol? _____

E♭ : vii°

11. Which chord matches the chord symbol? _____

f: V

12. Provide the correct chord symbol for each chord.

d: __   G: __   E♭: __   a: __   f♯: __   B♭: __

13. How many *major* triads occur in a major key? _____

14. How many *minor* triads occur in a major key? _____

15. On which scale degree do major triads occur in the harmonic minor scale? _____

16. Does the augmented triad occur in the major scale? _____

17. Does the diminished triad occur in both the major and harmonic minor scales? _____

Chapter 2.0
The Structure of Tonality

Chords built on the various scale degree differ not only in quality, but also possess different functions resulting from their position in the scale. Function means two things: the tendency for each chord to relate to the others in a consistent way, and the particular position each chord has in the edifice known as the "structure of tonality." Through chord function, harmony plays a role in the establishment of tonality. We may, in fact, speak of "harmonic tonality" — the result of consistent patterns of harmonic action, which cause a particular tone (or chord) to gain preeminence over the others. By noting the position of the chords in the tonal structure and examining their functions, we shall begin to understand the subtleties of the "language of harmony," often also identified as functional harmony.

2.1 Roman numerals are used chiefly for harmonic analysis. In addition to Roman numeral terminology, each triad has a proper name. The name in each case is either derived from the harmonic function of the triad or determined by its position in the scale. You will understand the full significance of these names later in this study, but the diagram below will shed some light upon their meaning and also the structure of tonality.

KEY OF G MAJOR

P5		P5
SUBDOMINANT	TONIC	DOMINANT
(IV)	(I)	(V)

The triad which is built on the first degree of the scale

tonic

(the keynote) is called the_____.

2.2 The word TONIC means "tone." This is the proper name given the triad built on the keynote of the scale. Since the keynote predominates over the remaining tones, *the tonic triad is the principal triad of the key.*

first

The tonic triad is built on the _____degree of the scale.

	2.3 Notice in frame 2.1 that the root of the DOMINANT triad is a perfect fifth *above* the keynote (G). Triads whose roots are related by the interval of a perfect fifth have a close relation to one another. This is due to the "fundamental" nature of the perfect fifth.*
	The triad whose root is a perfect fifth above the
dominant	keynote is called the _____.
	*In acoustics (the scientific study of sound), intervals are expressed by the ratio of frequencies between the two tones. The ratio of the perfect fifth is 3:2. This represents the simplest relationship of all intervals except the unison (1:1) and the octave (2:1). The student may read more about this by referring to the Acoustics section of the Bibliography.
	2.4 The *dominant* triad is so called because of its "dominant" position in the tonality. The root of the dominant triad is the interval of a
perfect fifth	_____above the keynote.
	2.5 Notice in Frame 2.1 that the root of the SUBDOMINANT triad is a perfect fifth *below* the keynote. The subdominant triad is so called because it occupies the same position *below* the tonic that the dominant has
above	_____ the tonic.
	2.6 The triad whose root is a perfect fifth *below* the
subdominant	keynote is called the_____.
	2.7 The *tonic*, *dominant*, and *subdominant* triads are the PRIMARY triads in any key. The importance of this statement will become clear as we progress. Since the tonic triad is built on the keynote (the center of the tonality), it has less harmonic activity than triads built on other degrees of the scale. It is the final chord of most compositions. Because of its position at the center of the tonality the tonic triad may be regarded as a "chord of repose." The three primary triads possess harmonic activity of ap-
False (*The tonic triad is relatively inactive.*)	proximately the same degree. (True/False)_____.
	2.8 The *dominant* and *subdominant* triads are both active and tend to progress to the *tonic*. The structure of tonality rests upon the three primary triads. This is due to the fundamental interval by which the roots of the dominant and subdominant chords are related to the tonic. What is this
Perfect fifth	interval? _____.

(1) Tonic

(2) Dominant

(3) Subdominant
(*Any order.*)

2.9 The structure of tonality rests upon the foundation of three chords. Name these chords.

(1) _____

(2) _____

(3) _____

---

e: i

2.10 Write on the staff the *tonic* triad in the key of E minor. Supply, also, the appropriate Roman numeral.

e: _____

B♭:   IV

2.11 Write on the staff the *subdominant* triad in the key of B-flat major. Supply, also, the appropriate Roman numeral.

B♭:   _____

---

g: V

2.12 Write on the staff the *dominant* triad in the key of G minor (*use the harmonic minor scale*). Supply, also, the appropriate Roman numeral.

g: _____

---

b♭:   iv

2.13 Write on the staff the *subdominant* triad in the key of B-flat minor (*use the harmonic minor scale*). Supply, also, the appropriate Roman numeral.

b♭:   _____

2.14 Write on the staff the *tonic* triad in the key of A major. Supply, also, the appropriate Roman numerals.

A: ____

2.15 Write on the staff the *dominant* triad in the key of F major. Supply, also, the appropriate Roman numeral.

F: ____

2.16 The triads which are built on tones midway between the tonic and dominant, and the tonic and subdominant, are called the MEDIANT and SUBDMEDIANT respectively.

KEY OF G MAJOR

SUBDOMINANT (IV)   TONIC (I)   DOMINANT (V)
SUBMEDIANT (vi)   MEDIANT (iii)

The triad whose root is on the sixth scale degree is called the submediant. The triad whose root is on the third

scale is called the _____.

mediant

2.17 Write the *mediant* and *submediant* triads in the key of A major.

MEDIANT   SUBMEDIANT

A: iii   vi

A: iii   vi

2.18   Write the *mediant* and *submediant* triads in the key of B minor *(use the harmonic minor scale).*

MEDIANT   SUBMEDIANT

b: III⁺   VI

b: III⁺   VI

2.19   Write the *mediant* and *submediant* triads in the key of G minor *(use the natural minor scale).*

MEDIANT   SUBMEDIANT

g: III⁺   VI

g: III⁺   VI

2.20   Write the *mediant* and *submediant* triads in the key of E-flat major.

MEDIANT   SUBMEDIANT

Eb: iii   vi

Eb: iii   vi

2.21   Five of the seven triads have been named. The relation of these triads to one another, and particularly to the key center, is reflected in the special order of the list below.

Write the name for each triad.

5th: Dominant

3rd: Mediant

1st: TONIC

6th: Submediant

4th: Subdominant

The triad on the 5th degree: _____

The triad on the 3rd degree: _____

THE TRIAD ON THE 1st DEGREE: _____

The triad on the 6th degree: _____

The triad on the 4th degree: _____

2.22 The two triads yet to be named are shown below:

KEY OF G MAJOR

LEADING TONE   TONIC   SUPERTONIC
(vii°)   (I)   (ii)

The triad whose root is a half-step *below* the tonic is called the LEADING TONE. The triad built on the second

supertonic

degree of the scale is called the _____ .

2.23 The prefix *super* means over, above, or on top of. Thus it is natural that the triad whose root is a second above the tonic should be called the SUPERTONIC.

The LEADING TONE triad derives its name from the fact that its root, being a half-step below the tonic, has a very strong tendency to "lead back" to the keynote.

Which of the triads below is the *supertonic* triad in

(4).

the key of E major? _____ .

(1)   (2)   (3)   (4)

2.24 Which of the triads below is the *leading tone* triad

(2).

in the key of F major? _____ .

(1)   (2)   (3)   (4)

2.25 Which of the triads below is the *leading tone* in

(4).
(See next frame)

the key of B-flat minor? _____ .

(1)   (2)   (3)   (4)

	2.26 You may have had difficulty choosing between items (2) and (4) in the preceding frame. The root of the leading tone triad, remember, is a *half-step* below the tonic. The triad A♭ CE♭ is a diatonic triad in B-flat natural (or melodic) minor, but it is NOT a leading tone triad. A triad built on the tone which is a *whole-step* below the tonic is called the SUBTONIC. The *subtonic* triad does not occur as a diatonic triad in either the major or harmonic minor scales.
True.	(True/False)_____
	2.27 The *leading tone* triad is built on a tone which is a half-step below the tonic. The *subtonic* triad is built on a tone
whole	which is a _____-step below the tonic.
	2.28 Which term is appropriate for the triad below?
Subtonic.	(Leading tone/Subtonic) _____
	<div align="center">KEY OF C MINOR</div>
	2.29 Which term is specifically for the triad below?
Leading tone.	(Leading tone/Subtonic) _____
	<div align="center">KEY OF F MINOR</div>
	2.30 Which of the triads below is the *leading tone* triad in
(2).	the key of D minor? _____
	(1) (2) (3)

(3).

2.31   Which of the triads below is the *subtonic* triad in the key of F-sharp minor? _____

2.32   The SUPERTONIC triad is located on the second degree of the scale.
    Write the *supertonic* triad in each of the keys indicated below:

G: ii   d: ii°   Ab: ii

2.33   Write the *supertonic* triad in each of the keys indicated below:

a: ii°   F: ii   c: ii°

2.34   The quality of the *supertonic* triad in a major key is minor. What is the quality of the *supertonic* triad in a

Diminished.

minor key (*harmonic minor scale*)? _____

C: I   ii   iii   IV

V   vi   vii°

2.35   Write the Roman numeral which is appropriate for each of the triads in the C major scale. (*An abbreviation of the proper name is given for each triad.*)

T   ST   M   SD   D   SM   LT

C: __   __   __   __   __   __   __

2.36 Write the Roman numeral which is appropriate for each of the triads in the C harmonic minor scale. (*Note the quality of each triad.*)

c: ᅳ ᅳ ᅳ ᅳ ᅳ ᅳ ᅳ

2.37 Write the Roman numeral which is appropriate for each of the triads in the C natural minor scale. (*Note the quality of each triad.*)

c: ᅳ ᅳ ᅳ ᅳ ᅳ ᅳ ᅳ

2.38 Write the proper name of each triad. (*Consider the seventh degree as being a half-step below the keynote.*)

1st: Tonic

2nd: Supertonic

3rd: Mediant

4th: Subdominant

5th: Dominant

6th: Submediant

7th: Leading tone

The triad on the 1st degree: _____

The triad on the 2nd degree: _____

The triad on the 3rd degree: _____

The triad on the 4th degree: _____

The triad on the 5th degree: _____

The triad on the 6th degree: _____

The triad on the 7th degree: _____

subtonic

2.39 A triad whose root is a whole-step below the keynote

is called the _____.

2.40   List the quality (major, minor, diminished or augmented) of the triads on each degree of a *major* scale.

1st: Major	The triad on the 1st degree: _____
2nd: Minor	The triad on the 2nd degree: _____
3rd: Minor	The triad on the 3rd degree: _____
4th: Major	The triad on the 4th degree: _____
5th: Major	The triad on the 5th degree: _____
6th: Minor	The triad on the 6th degree: _____
7th: Diminished	The triad on the 7th degree: _____

2.41   List the quality (as above) of the triad on each degree of the:

	harmonic minor scale	*natural minor scale*		*harmonic minor scale*	*natural minor scale**
1st:	Minor	Minor	The triad on the 1st degree: _____		
2nd:	Diminished	Diminished	The triad on the 2nd degree: _____		
3rd:	Augmented	Major	The triad on the 3rd degree: _____		
4th:	Minor	Minor	The triad on the 4th degree: _____		
5th:	Major	Minor	The triad on the 5th degree: _____		
6th:	Major	Major	The triad on the 6th degree: _____		
7th:	Diminished	Major	The triad on the 7th degree: _____		

*Common-practice composers use this form of the minor scale less often, but one should be alert to its usage.

B♭ DF	2.42 Spell the *tonic* triad in the key of B-flat major. _____
	2.43 Spell the *supertonic* triad in the key of G minor.
ACE♭	(*Use the notes of the harmonic minor scale.*) _____
D♯ F♯ A♯	2.44 Spell the *mediant* triad in the key of B major. _____
	2.45 Spell the *subdominant* triad in the key of G-sharp
C♯EG♯	minor. (*Use the notes of the harmonic minor scale.*)_____
E♭GB♭	2.46 Spell the *dominant* triad in the key of A-flat major. _____

D♭FA♭	2.47 Spell the *submediant* triad in the key of F minor. *(Use the notes of the harmonic minor scale.)* _____
CE♭G♭	2.48 Spell the *leading tone* triad in the key of D-flat major. _____
CEG♯	2.49 Spell the *mediant* triad in the key of A minor. *(Use the notes of the harmonic minor scale.)* _____
E♭GB♭	2.50 Spell the *mediant* triad in the key of C minor *(Use the notes of the natural minor scale.)* _____
A♯C♯E	2.51 Spell the *leading tone* triad in the key of B minor. *(Use the notes of the harmonic minor scale.)* _____
CEG	2.52 Spell the the *subtonic* triad in the key of D minor. *(Use the notes of the natural minor scale.)* _____

(*No response.*)	2.53 Do not continue unless the proper names and chord symbols are firmly fixed in your mind. The diagram below is yet another representation which may help.
	
	           4 *Subdominant* (IV)
	         3 *Mediant* (iii)
	      2 *Supertonic* (ii)
	    1 *Tonic* (I)
	     7 *Leading tone* (vii°)
	       6 *Submediant* (vi)
	         5 *Dominant* (V)

tonic	2.54 The tonic triad is built on the center of a tonality — the keynote. Harmonically the tonic triad is relatively static. The other diatonic triads are attracted to it and possess various degrees of activity. The precise relation each triad bears to the tonic (and to the other diatonic triads) is unique and the discovery of these relationships will occupy us for some time. First we shall observe some of the basic principles regarding the structure of tonality. The three primary triads of a tonality are the *tonic, dominant* and *subdominant*. Which of these triads possesses the least harmonic activity? The _____.

2.55   Inactive in most cases, the tonic triad is a relatively "neutral" chord. Most compositions begin and end with tonic harmony and a sense of relative repose accompanies the tonic triad whenever it appears within a harmonic phrase.

One of the most active triads is the *dominant*. This triad tends to demand resolution directly to the tonic.

Play the example below:

Beethoven, *Sonata*, Op. 2, No. 3

Allegro con brio

C: I   V

The harmonic movement is tonic-dominant — a basic progression in tonal music. Because it ends with an active chord (V), it sounds incomplete. We shall refer to such progressions as "opening" progressions.

The tonic and dominant are two of the three primary chords which provide the foundation for the structure of tonality. The root of the dominant triad is the interval of a

fifth

perfect _____above the tonic.

2.56   The "opening" progression (I-V) illustrated in the preceding frame is completed when the dominant seventh chord* progresses back to the tonic.

Beethoven, *Sonata*, Op. 2, No. 3

Allegro con brio

C: I   V

V⁷   I

Tonic and dominant harmonies provide the basis for many phrases. Does a series of chords ending on the dominant sound complete?

No.
(*The opening progression I-V is completed by returning to the tonic.*)

_____

*The dominant seventh chord possesses the same harmonic function as the dominant triad but has greater activity due to the dissonance provided by the seventh. This chord is treated fully in Chapter 10.0.

2.57   Two of the chords which constitute the tripodal foundation of the structure of tonality are the *tonic* and *dominant*; the third is the SUBDOMINANT.

Play the example below:

Mozart, *Sonata*, K. 311

The basic harmonic movement in this example is I-IV. This is another of the common "opening" progressions. The character of the subdominant chord is quite different from that of the dominant. The need for resolution into the tonic is not as strong for the subdominant as for the dominant.

No.
(*The tonic chord is required to produce a sense of finality.*)

Does the phrase above end with a sense of finality? _____

2.58   The "opening" progression I-IV is often completed by IV-I.

Play the example below:

Schumann, *Album for the Young*, Op. 68, No. 10

tonic

Both of the "opening" progressions I-V and I-IV are completed by a return to the _____ triad.

■ 2.59   The subdominant chord often progresses to the dominant rather than returning at once to the tonic.

Play the example below:

Bach, Chorale: *In allen meinen Taten*

F: I   IV   V

This example shows another of the basic harmonic progressions (IV-V). The subdominant chord progresses as naturally to the dominant as to the tonic.

The subdominant chord may return immediately to the

dominant (V)

tonic or it may progress to the _____.

2.60   Below is a list of the three *basic* progressions:

	OPENING	COMPLETION
(1)	I-V	V-I
(2)	I-IV	IV-I
(3)	(I) IV-V	V-I

Despite their seeming simplicity, these harmonic relations constitute the basic harmonic underpinning of much eighteenth and nineteenth century music.

Complete, in terms of the basic progressions, the statement below (*use Roman numerals*):

IV (or to) V
(*Any order.*)

The tonic (I) can progress to_____or to_____.

2.61   Complete, in terms of the basic harmonic progressions, the statement below (*use Roman numerals*):

I (or to) V
(*Any order.*)

The subdominant (IV) can progress to _____or to _____.

tonic (I)	**2.62** To what triad is the dominant most likely to progress? The _____. Note: The dominant moving to the subdominant is not considered a progression but rather a retrogression; see Frames 7.2–.5, 7.17 for further comment.
diminished	**2.63** The PRIMARY triads in any key are the tonic, subdominant and dominant triads. The remaining triads (supertonic, mediant, submediant and leading tone) are SECONDARY triads. The *primary* triads in any major key are all major triads. The *secondary* triads (in major) are either minor or _____.
ii, iii (and) vi (*Any order.*)	**2.64** List with Roman numerals the three triads (in major) which are *minor* in quality. _____,_____ and_____.

I, IV, (and) V
 	
 ii, iii, vi, (and) vii°
 (*Any order.*)
	2.65 Complete the chart below:
	
	     Primary triads: _____,_____ and_____.
	
	     Secondary triads: _____,_____, _____ and _____.

i (and) iv (*Any order.*)	**2.65** Two of the primary triads (in harmonic minor) are minor in quality. List these triads: _____ and _____.
ii° (and) vii° (*Any order.*)	**2.67** Two of the secondary triads (in harmonic minor) are diminished. List these triads: _____ and_____.
perfect fifth	**2.68** The primary triads provide the foundation for the structure of tonality. This is due to the fundamental intervallic relationship of the the perfect fifth between their roots. The roots of the dominant and subdominant triads are related to the tonic by the interval of a _____.

2.69   The relation which the various secondary triads bear to the tonic is shown here:

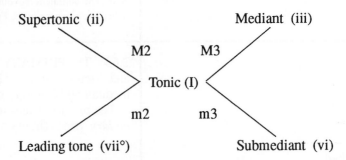

(Major Tonality)

Supertonic (ii)   Mediant (iii)

M2   M3

Tonic (I)

m2   m3

Leading tone (vii°)   Submediant (vi)

The secondary triads are related to the tonic by

third

intervals of the second or _____.

2.70   Music in which the primary triads are emphasized tends to sound "positive" and "strong." The over-use of these triads, however, can result in an excessively "stable" or "dull" effect. Secondary triads are used to provide tonal variety and to give additional color to the harmony.

Play and compare the two progressions below:

(1)

G: I   vi   IV   V   I

(2)

G: I   vi   ii   iii   I

(1)
(There is no doubt that (2) is in G major; but, since minor (secondary) triads predominate, the impression of a major key is weakened.)

Which of these examples gives the stronger sense of

the key of G major? (1) or (2) _____.

2.71   Observe the relation of secondary triads to the tonic in *harmonic minor* as follows:

KEY OF G MINOR
(Harmonic Minor Scale)

g: vii°   ii°   i   III⁺   VI

Minor third.	By what interval is the *mediant* triad related to the tonic in harmonic minor? (*Be specific.*) _____
Major third.	2.72 By what interval is the submediant triad related to the tonic in harmonic minor? _____
major	2.73 In harmonic minor the root of the *mediant* triad is a minor third above the tonic. In major the root of the *mediant* triad is a _____ third above the tonic.
minor	2.74 In harmonic minor the root of the *submediant* triad is a major third below the tonic. In major the root of the *submediant* triad is a _____ third below the tonic.
No. (*In major the supertonic triad is minor; but it is diminished in harmonic minor.*)	2.75 The root of the *supertonic* triad is related to the tonic by the interval of a major second in both major and minor. Is the quality of this triad the same in major as it is in (harmonic) minor? _____
Yes, (*Both are diminished.*)	2.76 The root of the *leading tone* triad is related to the tonic by the interval of a minor second in both major and harmonic minor. Is the quality of this triad the same in each case? _____
	2.77 Each of the secondary triads associates with a specific primary triad. *Study the diagram below:* KEY OF C MAJOR

Primary: I   IV   V
Secondary: vi   ii   iii   vii°

thirds	Secondary triads are used as substitutes for the primary triads with which they are associated and have similar harmonic functions. What are the intervals between the roots of primary triads and their secondary triads? Major and minor_____.

I   - vi
 	
IV - ii
 	
V - iii, vii°
	2.78 Each secondary triad is located a third *below* its primary triad with the exception of the leading tone (vii°). The harmonic functions of the leading tone and dominant triads are practically identical.* Each tends to progress directly to the tonic.
	
	Indicate with Roman numerals the secondary triad(s) associated with each primary triad.
	
	PRIMARY TRIADS SECONDARY TRIADS
	
	      I - _____
	
	     IV - _____
	
	      V - _____
	
	_____
	*The leading tone triad is often considered to be a dominant seventh chord with the root omitted.

subdominant (IV)	2.79 Which primary triad is associated with the supertonic triad? The _____triad.
tonic (I)	2.80 Which primary triad is associated with the submediant triad? The _____triad.
dominant (V)	2.81 Which primary triad is associated with the mediant triad? The _____triad.
leading tone (vii°)	2.82 Which secondary triad has practically the same harmonic function as the dominant? The_____ _____triad.

Summary

Roman numerals are used chiefly for harmonic analysis, while proper names (*tonic, supertonic, etc.*) are used when speaking or writing. Since both Roman numerals and proper names will be used throughout this study, it is necessary for you to become fluent in both methods of identifying chords. Whereas proper names do not reveal the quality of triads, Roman numerals do. So you must be especially careful to choose the form of Roman numeral appropriate to the quality of the triad to be represented.

The three primary triads — I, IV and V — provide the foundation for the structure of tonality. The roots of the dominant and subdominant triads are related to the tonic by the interval of a perfect fifth. This interval is the "simplest" (see Frame 2.3) by which different chords can be related. This relationship accounts for the fundamental role which these triads play in the establishment of tonality. The tonic (I) is the center of the tonality; the dominant (V) is a perfect fifth *above* the tonic; and the subdominant (IV) is a perfect fifth *below* the tonic.

With respect to primary triads there are three basic harmonic progressions: I-V, I-IV and IV-V. Each of these is an "opening" progression, which is completed by harmonic movement back to the tonic. Harmonic phrases usually begin on, and ultimately return to the tonic. Thus some typical *basic* harmonic phrases are: I-V-I, I-IV-I and I-IV-V-I.

Secondary triads are used as substitutes for primary triads for the sake of tonal variety. With only one exception, the roots of secondary triads are the interval of a third *below* the primary triads to which they relate. The exception is the leading tone triad (vii°) whose root is located a third *above* the dominant.

The harmonic function of secondary triads is similar to that of the primary triads with which they are associated. This association is strongest in the case of the dominant and leading tone triads, for each of these triads can progress directy to the tonic. The difference between them is due not to their function, but to their quality (the dominant is major, the leading tone is diminished).

The symmetrical structure of tonality is represented in the diagram below. The tonic (I) is the center of the structure with the other two primary triads (V and IV) spaced a perfect fifth above and below. The entire structure is based on thirds.

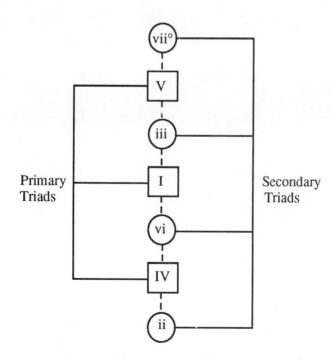

Mastery Frames

---

(5) Dominant (4) Subdominant (1) Tonic (2.1–.6)	2–1 Write the proper name for triads built on the indicated scale degrees. *Scale Degree* *Proper Name* (5) _____ (4) _____ (1) _____
primary (2.1–.15)	2–2 All of the triads in the preceding frame are (primary/ secondary) _____triads.
(Mediant) 3rd (Submediant) 6th (2.16–.21)	2–3 Indicate the scale degree on which each triad is built. Mediant _____ Submediant _____
(7) Leading tone (2) Supertonic (2.22–.34)	2–4 Write the proper name for the triads built on the indicated scale degrees. *Scale Degree* *Proper Name* (7) _____ (2) _____
 Eb: I ii iii IV V vi vii° (2.35)	2–5 Write the appropriate Roman numeral for each triad. Eb: __ __ __ __ __ __ __

f#:   i   ii°   III⁺   iv

V   VI   vii°

(2.36)

2–6 Write the appropriate Roman numeral for each triad.

f#: __   __   __   __   __   __   __

Dominant.

(2.54)

2–7 Which of the two triads below is more active?

_____

Tonic   Dominant

---

tonic (I)

(2.55–.59)

2–8 "Opening" harmonic progressions such as I-V or I-IV are completed by eventually progressing to the

_____.

P

S

S

P

P

S

S   (2.62–.66)

2–9 Identify each triad as either primary (P), or Secondary (S).

Tonic   _____

Supertonic   _____

Mediant   _____

Subdominant   _____

Dominant   _____

Submediant   _____

Leading tone   _____

---

vi

ii

iii, vii°   (2.6–.77)

2–10 Indicate with Roman numerals the secondary triad(s) associated with each primary triad.

Primary Triad   Secondary Triads

I   _____

IV   _____

V   _____

Supplementary Assignments

ASSIGNMENT 2–1   Name _____

1. Provide the proper names for the three triads represented by the Roman numerals below.

    V _____

    I _____

    IV _____

2. Name the secondary triad(s) that relate to each of the primary triads below (use proper names).

    V _____

    I _____

    IV _____

3. Name the triad which rests on the tonal center. _____

4. The dominant triad is built on the _____ scale degree.

5. Which triad has the same position below the tonal center that the dominant has above? _____

6. Upon which scale degrees are secondary triads built? _____

7. Explain the meaning of the terms "mediant" and "submediant". _____

    _____

8. The triad built on the seventh scale degree is called the _____

9. Draw a diagram which shows your conception of the structure of tonality.

10. Write the proper Roman numeral for each triad.

g: __   __   __   __   __

11. Write the proper Roman numeral for each triad.

    G: __   __   __   __   __

12. Indicate the scale degree on which each chord is built.

     Subdominant _____

     Mediant _____

     Supertonic _____

     Tonic _____

     Leading tone _____

     Submediant _____

     Dominant _____

13. List the scale degree of which minor triads occur in a major tonality. _____

     _____

14. Roots of primary and secondary triads are related by the interval of a _____.

15. Show with chord symbols the three primary triads and the secondary triad(s) related to each.

              Primary triads   Secondary triads

     _____   _____

     _____   _____

     _____   _____

ASSIGNMENT 2–2   Name _____

1.   What is the name of the triad that is built on the tonal center of a key? _____

2.   Write a single line melody based on the indicated harmony.

3.   Describe the effect of the harmony underlying the melody you wrote in question 2.

   _____

   _____

4   Use Roman numerals to show three "opening" harmonic progressions.

   _____   _____   _____

5.   What is meant by a "closing" progression? _____

   _____

6.   Write a single line melody based on the indicated chord progression.

7.   Is the harmonic progression in question 6 an "opening" or a "closing" progression? _____

8.   Write a single line melody based on the indicated harmonic progression.

9.   Is the harmonic progression in question 8 an "opening" or a "closing" progression? _____

10. Write a single line melody based on the indicated harmonic progression.

     e: i   iv   V   i

11. Write a single line melody based on the indicated harmonic progression.

     F: I   —   IV   V

12. What term is used to describe the harmonic progression above? _____

13. Which progression is most conclusive? _____

     a. I-IV
     b. IV-V
     c. V-iii
     d. V-I
     e. V-vi

14. Which progression is most conclusive? _____

     a. I-IV
     b. vii°-vi
     c. V-i
     d. V-iii
     e. V-vi
     f. IV-V

15. Write Roman numerals to identify the chords that underly the melody.

     d: __   __   __   __

Chapter 3.0
Triads in Root Position: Doubling and Spacing

With this chapter we shall begin to master the techniques of writing chords and leading voices smoothly from one chord to another. The first step is to become acquainted with "figured bass" symbols. These symbols constitute a form of shorthand notation and also are used for analysis. Next we shall focus on principles of doubling and spacing of triads in root position. The basis for this work will be the four-voice chorus. Although this aspect of the study of harmony is rather "mechanical," it nevertheless is vital, both to effective writing and the understanding of factors which affect liner action in harmonic music. The latter, especially, contributes to effective performance and fluent reading.

3.1   A triad is in ROOT POSITION if its root is the lowest tone.

In each of the triads above, the root is the lowest tone.

These triads are in _____ position.

root

3.2   Write triads in root position as directed. (Capital letter = major; lower case letter = minor.)

(1)   (2)   (3)

Eb   g   B

(1)   (2)   (3)

3.3   Write triads in root position as directed.

(1)   (2)   (3)

c#   E   g#

(1)   (2)   (3)

(2).

3.4 Which of the triads below is in root position? _____

3.5 The intervals of a fifth and third occur over the lowest tone of a triad in root position. These intervals sometimes are represented by the numbers 5 and 3. These are called FIGURED BASS SYMBOLS.*

(*Note that the larger number is always placed above the smaller.*)

Figured bass symbols are merely a listing of the intervals which occur above the lowest note. The numbers 5 and 3 beneath

root

a note indicate a triad in _____position.

---

*Figured bass symbols were widely used during the baroque era as a shorthand notation for players of keyboard instruments. They will be used here for the purpose of analysis and as an aid in teaching the principles of part writing.

3.6 Accidentals applied to the upper notes are shown in the figured bass.*

The symbol ♭5 means that the note a fifth above the lowest

flatted
(*or lowered a half-step*)

note is _____.

---

*Accidentals applied to the lowest note, or to its duplication one or more octaves higher are not indicated.

3.7 Figured bass is a shorthand system of indicating notes above the bass (the lowest part). There are several special signs and conventions which must be learned in connection with the use of figured bass symbols.

A slash through a number means that the note representsd by the number is RAISED a half-step.

Observe the used of this sign below:

Yes.
(*But see the next frame.*)

Does the symbol #5 mean the same as the symbol 5̸?_____

3.8   The figured bass symbols 5̸ and 3̸ do not always refer to the use of sharps (#). The raising of a tone by a half-step is sometines accomplished by a natural (♮), or a double-sharp (×). The key signature (if any) must be taken into account. Compare the three triads below:

In (1) the fifth of the triad has been raised a half-step by the use of a natural (♮); in (2) a sharp (#) has been used to produce the same result; in (3̸) a double-sharp (×) has been used.

The symbol 3̸ might be used in place of *any* of the follow

True.

ing: × 3, #3, or ♮3. (True/False) _____

3.9   Check (√) the correct option:

1.   A slash through a number means that the note represented by the number is raised a half-step.
2.   A slash through a number calls for a sharp.
True statements:

(1) √

(1) _____   (2) _____   Both _____ Neither_____

3.10   Write the triads and apply accidentals as indicated by the figured bass symbols.

3.11   Write the triads and apply accidentals as indicated by the figured bass symbols.

3.12   Notice in (3) of the preceding frame that the raised fifth is indicated by showing the actual accidental used. Alterations often are indicated in this manner. You should experience no difficulty in interpreting such symbols if you will merely apply accidentals exactly as directed by the figured bass.

Write the triads and apply accidentals as directed.

3.13   An accidental NOT associated with a number refers to the interval of a *third* above the lowest note.

Examine carefully the three examples below:

An alteration of the third above the lowest note may be indicat-

accidental   ed merely by using the appropriate_____.

root

3.14   Write the triad as indicated by the figured bass symbols.

3.15   Write the triads as indicated by the figured bass symbols.

3.16   Since figured bass symbols are a shorthand method of indicating chord structures, use only those figures which are necessary. Generally no figuration is given for a triad in root position except to show the alteration (by accidental) of either the third or fifth of the triad.

In (1) no figuration is necessary as neither the third nor the fifth is altered; a sharp is used in (2) to show that the third is raised from C to C-sharp; the symbol ♭5 is used in (3) to show the alteration of E to E-flat; the figured 5̸ and ♯ are used in (4) to show that the fifth and third are both raised a half-step.

No figuration under a bass note indicates the following:

1   No accidentals appear in the upper parts.

2.   The sonority is a triad in _____position.

3.17   Write the triads as indicated by the figured bass symbols.

3.18   Write the triads as indicated by the figured bass symbols.

(1)   (2)   (3)

3.19   Write the figured bass symbols beneath each triad as needed.

(1)   (2)   (3)

3.20   Write figured bass symbols beneath each triad as needed.

(1)   (2)   (3)

3.21   Write figured bass symbols beneath each triad as needed.

(1)   (2)   (3)

3.22   Figured bass symbols provide a simple way to indicate chord sonorities and have many other uses, as we shall see later. Interpreting these symbols is easy, if you remember this fact: *Figured bass symbols always indicate intervals above the lowest voice; they are a record of intervals from the bass upward.*

Other important points to remember are these:

1. A triad in root position usually requires no figuration unless either the third or fifth is altered.

2. A slash through a number means that the note represented by the number is raised a half-step.

(No response.)

3. An accidental in the figured bass which is not associated with a number refers to the interval of a third above the bass.

3.23   Now let us turn to the specific techniques of *doubling* (assignment of same chord member to two or more voices) and *spacing* (placement of the chord members).

Since triads consist of three tones, no problem of doubling exists if these tones are to be given to three instruments or voices, or if a three-part texture is used in writing for a keyboard instrument. In such cases the triads are complete if the root is given to one part, the third to another and the fifth to still another.

When working with triads, doubling is generally not a problem

three

unless more than _____ instrument or voices are used.

3.24   Much of the music composed since the middle of the eighteenth century is based on a four-part texture. The utility of this texture has been proved by more that two centuries of use. It provides an agreeable sonority without imposing undue problems of doubling, or of voice leading.

The texture which has prevailed as the basis of much of the music

four

for the last 200 years is the _____ -part texture.

3.25   Although this study is not devoted exclusively to four-part writing, this texture is so prevalent in music of the baroque, classical and romantic eras that we must spend a considerable amount of time studying it.

The more mechanical aspects of part writing will be presented in terms of the four-part chorus, which consists of the soprano, alto, tenor and bass voices. It is convenient to use this medium as a basis for our study since it expresses clearly the four-part texture and the principles upon which our attention is to be focused usually are not clouded by other factors, as often is the case in music for the paino or instrumental ensembles.

Name the voices which constitute the four-part chorus.

(1)   Soprano   (3)   Tenor

(2)   Alto   (4)   Bass

(Any order.)

(1) _____   (3) _____

(2) _____   (4) _____

3.26   You must learn the approximate range for each of the voices.

Soprano   Alto

Tenor   Bass

o = practical range
● = possible range

It is impossible to establish absolute limits for voices. Individual singers vary, and such factors as the dynamic level and the color desired in a given passage help determine the appropriateness of particular tones. Generally, though, you should keep the voices within the practical ranges given above.

(*Study these ranges before continuing with the next frame.*)

(*No response*)

3.27   Circle the notes which are *outside* the possible range of the *soprano* voice.

(2)   (4)   (1)   (2)   (3)   (4)

3.28   Circle the note which are *outside* the possible range of the *alto* voice.

(1)   (3)   (1)   (2)   (3)   (4)

(2)   **(3)**

3.29 Circle the notes which are *outside* the possible range of the *tenor* voice.

(1)   (2)   (3)   (4)

(3)

3.30 Circle the notes which are *outside* the possible range of the *bass* voice.

(1)   (2)   (3)   (4)

3.31 The voices of the four-part chorus are notated in several configurations on the grand staff as illustrated below:

Soprano

Alto

Tenor

Bass

The *soprano* is the highest voice and is always notated on the treble staff with stems going up; the *alto* is the next highest voice and is always notated on the treble staff with stems going down.

The *tenor* and *bass* voices are notated on the bass staff. Upward stems are always used by the tenor and downward stems are always used by the bass

Name two voices which use upward stems.

(1) Soprano   (2) Tenor

(Any order.)

(1) _____   (2) _____

(1) Alto   (2) Bass

(Any order.)

3.32 Name the two voices which use downward stems.

(1) _____   (2) _____

(1)   (2)   (3)

3.33   Place stems correctly on the notes of each chord.

3.34   Sometimes two voices sing the same pitch (doubling); i.e., they are said to "double" each other. Notice how this is notated.

(1)   (2)   (3)

When two voices are to sing the same pitch, two stems are attached to one notehead, or two notes are used when there are whole notes involved. When two voices on different staves sing the same pitch (alto and tenor), it is necessary to write both notes. In two of the above examples the upward stems attached to the notes on the bass staff represent the tenor voice; downward stems

bass

represent the _____ voice.

3.35   In the normal distribution of voices the soprano takes the highest pitch, the alto the next highest, the tenor the next, and the bass takes the lowest pitch.
   When the normal distrubution of voices is not observed, the parts are said to be "crossed." Which two voices are "crossed" in the example below?

alto (and) tenor

The _____ and_____.

soprano (and) alto	3.36 Which two voices are "crossed" in the example below? The _____ and _____.
	3.37 The impetus of melodic writing will cause an occasional crossing of voices in more advanced writing. For the present, however, normal distribution should be observed. List the voices in their normal distribution *from the highest to the lowest.*
(1) Soprano	(1) _____
(2) Alto	(2) _____
(3) Tenor	(3) _____
(4) Bass	(4) _____
bass	3.38 The "spacing" of a chord concerns primarily the intervals which separate the three upper voices (soprano, alto, and tenor) from one another. Which of the four voices can *not* be called an upper voice? The _____.
	3.39 The most satisfactory spacing of a chord usually requires that the intervals which separate the soprano and alto, and the alto and tenor, should not exceed an octave. In (1) and (2) below, no two adjacent upper voices are separated by an interval greater than an octave. In (3), however, the interval between the tenor and alto voices is an eleventh. If carried on for several chords this type of spacing would cause an "empty" effect, so it should be avoided.

octave

| | What is the largest interval by which adjacent upper voices should be separated? The _____. |

(2).
(There is a 10th between the soprano and alto.)

3.40   In which case below is there an excessive interval between adjacent upper voices? _____

Note: *Not all of the triad tones above are in root position.*

(1).
(There is a 10th between the alto and tenor.)

3.41   In which case below is there an excessive interval between adjacent upper voices? _____

3.42   Notice in (3) of the preceding frame that the interval between the tenor and bass is greater than an octave. *This is satisfactory.* An interval as large as a twelfth may separate the tenor from the bass without resulting in an unpleasant sonority. It is the upper voices (*soprano, alto* and *tenor*) which must observe the octave limitation.

Are there any irregularities in the spacing of the following chords? _____

No.

Note: *Not all of the triad tones above are in root position.*

3.43   Are there any irregularities in the spacing of the

chords below? _____

Yes.
*(In (2) there is more than an octave be-
tween the alto and tenor.)*

Note: *Not all of the triad tones above are in root position.*

3.44   If the three tones of a triad are to be given to four voices, it is
evident that one of the tones must be doubled. Doubled tones are
bracketed in the examples below. In each case the triad tone which is

doubled is the (root/third/fifth)_____.

root

THE C MAJOR TRIAD

3.45 Draw brackets (as in the preceding frame) to indicate the doubled tones is each triad.

3.46 The preceding two frames have demonstrated the usual doubling for triads in root position.
   Learn this principle:

When a triad is in root position the BASS is usually doubled.

If the bass is doubled in a root position triad, which

triad tone is doubled? The (root/third/fifth) _____.

root

3.47 When a triad is in root position the BASS is doubled by one of the upper voices. The remaining two voices take the third and fifth of the triad.
   A triad in root position will have two roots, one third

and one _____.

fifth

3.48 Add the alto and tenor voices to complete each chord.

Before looking at the answers check carefully each of the following items:
1. Is the bass doubled?
2. Are the third and fifth present?
3. Are the voices in normal distribution?
4. Is the interval between adjacent upper voices limited to an octave?
5. Are figured bass symbols realized correctly?

3.49   Add the alto and tenor voices to complete each chord.

(Before looking at the answers check carefully the five items stated in the preceding frame.)

3.50   Add the alto and tenor voices to complete each chord.

(Before looking at the answers check carefully the five items stated in Frame 3.48.)

Incorrect doubling
(There are two thirds.)

3.51   What is the part writing error in the chord below?

_____

The soprano and alto are more than an octave apart.

3.52   What is the part writing error in the chord below?

_____

_____

Incorrect doubling.

(*There is no fifth in the chord.*)

3.53   What is the part writing error in the chord below?

_____

3.54   In the example below, the tones of the C major triad have been spaced two different ways.

(1)   (2)

The spacing in (1) is called CLOSE STRUCTURE, and the spacing in (2) is called OPEN STRUCTURE.

Close and *open* structure concern the way the three upper voices are spaced. The spacing of triad tones results in two

close (and) open

(*Any order.*)

kinds of structures: these are called _____ and

_____structure.

3.55   Observe in (1) of the preceding frame that the upper voices are as *close* together as they can be. Reading down from the soprano each successive voice takes the next available chord tone.

> Soprano - C
> Alto   - G
> Tenor   - E

There are no vacant triad tones between the upper

voices when a triad is in _____ structure.

close

3.56   When a triad is in *open* structure there is a vacant triad tone between the soprano and alto, and between the alto and tenor voices. This causes the interval between the soprano and tenor voices to be greater than an octave.

The example below shows a chord in *open* structure. Indicate (with a black notehead) the *unoccupied* triad tone between each of the three upper voices.

THE A MINOR TRIAD

Write here

3.57   Below is another example of *open* structure. Indicate (with a black notehead) the *unoccupied* triad tone between each of the three upper voices.

THE F MAJOR TRIAD

Write here

3.58   If, when reading down from the soprano, you find that each successive voice (soprano, alto and tenor) takes the next available

triad tone, the chord is in _____ structure.

close

3.59   Which of the chords below are in *close* structure?

(1) and (4).

_____

3.60   Which of the chords below are in *close* structure?

(2) and (4).

_____

3.61   Write the alto and tenor voices so that each chord is in *close* structure.

3.62 Write the alto and tenor voices so that each chord is in *close* structure.

3.63 Write the alto and tenor voices so that each chord is in *close* structure.

(2)

3.64 Write the alto and tenor voices so that each chord is in *close* structure.

(If you have made no more that four errors in the last six frames you may skip to Frame 3.73.)

3.65   If you have made mistakes in translating the figure bass symbols, you should review Frames 3.5–.22.

Review, also, the principles of doubling and spacing stated below:

1.   When a triad is in root position double the bass (root).
2.   A triad in root position should have two roots, one third and one fifth.
3.   The voices should be distributed normally (the highest tone given to the soprano, the next highest to the alto, the next to the tenor and the lowest to the bass).
4.   There should not be more than an octave between any of the upper voices.
5.   *Close* structure means that the three upper voices take successive triad tones. These voices are as close together as the triad permits.

(No response.)

---

(4).

3.66   Which of the chords is in *close* structure? _____

---

(2).

3.67   Which of the chords is NOT in close structure? _____

Crossed voices (*The tenor is higher than the alto.*)	3.68 What part writing error is illustrated below?_____ ♭5 ♭3
The interval between the alto and tenor is larger that an octave.	3.69 What part writing error is illustrated below?_____ _____ ♭
The figured bass symbol 5̸ has not been realized (*F-sharp is needed*).	3.70 What part writing error is illustrated below?_____ _____ 5̸ ♯
(1) (2) (3)	3.71 Write the alto and tenor voices so that each chord is in *close* structure. (1) (2) (3) ♭5

3.72   Write the alto and tenor voices so that each chord is in *close* structure.

(1)   (2)   (3)

♭5   3

open

3.73   If there is a vacant triad tone between each of the

three upper voices, the chord is in _____structure.

(3) and (4).

3.74   Which of the chords below are in *open* structure?

_____.

(1)   (2)   (3)   (4)

♭   3

(1) and (3)

3.75   Which of the chords below are in *open* structure?

_____.

(1)   (2)   (3)   (4)

♭5   #   3
#

3.76 Write the alto and tenor voices so that each chord is in *open* structure.

3.77 Write the alto and tenor voices so that each chord is in *open* structure.

3.78 Write the alto and tenor voices so that each chord is in *open* structure.

3.79   Write the alto and tenor voices so that each chord is in *open* structure.

3.80   Write the alto and tenor voices so that each chord is in *open* structure.

3.81   Due to the location of the given notes, each of the chords below can be written only one way without producing irregularities in part writing.

Write the alto and tenor voices choosing the structure (close or open) which is correct in each case.

(If your solutions do not agree with the ones given, examine your work to find the errors, and consult your instructor if necessary.)

3.82   Continue as in the preceding frame.

(No response.)

3.83   A triad is in *root position* when the root is in the lowest voice. When the three tones of a triad are given to four instruments or voices, one of the tones must be doubled. The doubled tone usually is in the lowest voice (the root).

Tones are spaced to provide a variety of sonorities. By spacing the three upper voices close together a "compact" or "sonorous" effect results. This is called *close structure*. A less "compact" (more "open") effect results if the tones are spread apart by leaving a triad tone vacant between each of the three upper voices. This is called *open structure*. The choice between these two structures is made on the basis of the sonority desired, or is dictated by the practical necessity of keeping the voices within their proper ranges.

Both √

3.84   Check (√) the correct option:

1.   In close structure the three upper voices are as close together as the triad allows.

2.   In open structure there is a vacant triad tone between the soprano and alto, and between the alto and tenor.

True statements:

(1) _____   (2) _____   Both _____   Neither _____

■   3.85   The principles of doubling and spacing have been presented in terms of the four-part chorus. Most music based on a four-part texture will display these principles. Music for the piano, instrumental ensembles, and even the orchestra often is based on a four-part texture (sometimes expanded by octave doubling).

    Examine the chords marked with asterisks (*) in the following example:

Handel, *Sarabande*

root   Which triad tone is doubled in each instance? The _____.

Close.   3.86   Which of the two structures is demonstrated in the preceding frame? (Open/Close) _____.

Open.   ■   3.87   Which of the two structures is demonstrated by the chords marked with asterisks below? (Open/Closed) _____.

Brahms, *Ein deutsches Requiem*, Op. 45, IV

---

bass   3.88   Which voice (soprano, alto, tenor or base) is doubled when a triad is in root position? The _____.

Summary

If the three upper voices are spaced as close together as possible the chord is in *close* structure. *Open* structue results when there is a vacant chord tone between the soprano and alto, and the alto and tenor voices. In this case the interval between the soprano and tenor voices is greater than an octave. Close structure produces a more "compact" sound than open structure.

The basic principles which govern the doubling and spacing of triads in root position are listed below:

1. The voices should be kept within their practical ranges.

2. The voices should be in normal distribution (avoid crossed voices).

3. The interval between any two adjacent upper voices should not exceed an octave.

4. The bass is usually doubled in four-part writing.

Figured bass symbols are used to quickly convey certain musical facts about chordal sturctures. They may also be used to indicate melodic movement. The symbols consist mainly of numbers, accidentals, and other signs. Used for whatever purpose, they actually indicate nothing more than intervals above the lowest sounding note.

The figured bass symbols introduced in this chapter are summarized below:

(1)   The numbers 5 and 3 indicate a 5th and a 3rd above the note G. The result is a triad in root position.

(2)   The figure ♯3 indicates the note G-sharp. The result is an E major triad.

(3)   Used as a figured bass symbol, an accidental that stands alone (and is not associated with a number) affects the note that is a third above the bass, in this case A-flat. The result is an F minor triad.

(4)   A slash (/) through a number causes the note represented by the number to be raised a half-step. In this case both the fifth and third above the bass are raised a half-step by the use of sharps.

(5)   Here a natural is used to raise the third above the bass. (The natural cancels the A-flat in the key signature.)

Mastery Frames

root
(3.1–.4)

3–1   When the root of a triad is in the lowest voice, the

triad is in _____position.

3–2   Write triads in root position as directed.

(1)   (2)   (3)

D   ab   F♯

(3.1–.4)

3–3   Write the triad as indicated by the figured bass symbols.

(1)   (2)   (3)

(3.5–.22)

3–4   Write the figured bass symbols beneath each triad as needed.

(1)   (2)   (3)

(3.5–.22)

3–5 Write the figured bass symbols beneath each triad as needed.

(1)   (2)   (3)

(3.5–.22)

root (bass)

(3.44–.45)

3–6 In four-part writing, a triad in root position will

usually have the _____ doubled.

(1), (3).

3–7 Which chords have *incorrect* doubling? _____

(1)   (2)   (3)   (4)

(3.44–.47)

(4).

3–8 List the chord(s) in the preceding frame that is in *close*

structure. _____

(3.54–.57)

octave

(3.39)

3–9 Adjacent upper voices in general should not be spaced

more than the interval of a(n) _____ apart.

Supplementary Assignments

ASSIGNMENT 3–1   Name_____

1. Which of the triads are in root position? _____

2. Write triads in root position as directed.(Capital letter = major; lower case letter = minor.)

3. Write the triads indicated by the figured bass symbols.

4.   Supply the figured bass symbols where needed.

5.   Indicate the approximate range for each voice of the four-part chorus.

6.   Which chords are in *close* structure? _____

7.   What interval should not be exceeded when spacing adjacent upper voices? _____

8.   An interval as large as a(n) _____ may separate the lowest two voices.

ASSIGNMENT 3–2   Name _____

1.   Write the missing two voices for each chord. (*Use close structure.*)

2.   Write the missing two voices for each chord. (*Use open structure.*)

3.   Choose one or more of the options for each example.

    (A) _____ (B) _____ (C) _____ (D) _____ (E) _____

    (1)   Crossed voices   (4)   Voice out of normal range

    (2)   Incorrect spacing   (5)   No error

    (3)   Incorrect doubling

4. Supply the figured bass symbols for each chord.

5. Write the three upper voices using either open or close structure. Observe all rules of doubling and spacing.

Chapter 4.0
Triads in Root Position: Voice Leading

Chords are the result of several voices sounding simultaneously. When several chords occur in succession it is desirable that each voice produce an agreeable melodic line. With reference to tonal harmony in the traditional styles of the eighteenth and nineteenth centuries this means that the voices should lead smoothly (with few leaps) from one chord to the next. The principles of voice leading presented in this chapter will serve as guide lines for the effective movement of voices.

4.1 Since harmony consists of several melodic lines sounding together to produce chords, it is important to know how voices relate to one another in terms of relative motion. There are four kinds of relative motion: *similar, parallel, oblique and contrary*. We shall examine each of these separately.

Below are three examples of SIMILAR motion:

Voices which move in similar motion move in the same direction (up or down), but *not by the same interval*. In (1), for example, the upper voices ascends a second while the lower voice ascends a third. This is reflected by the harmonic intervals produced by the two voices (a sixth followed by a fifth).

In *similar* motion the voices move in the same direction but not

| interval | by the same _____. |

4.2 Write the notes indicated by the figured bass symbols.

similar

4.3   Each of the examples in the preceding frame

demonstrates _____motion.

---

(1)   (2)   (3)

6   6   5   6   3   5

4.4   Write the notes indicated by the figured bass symbols.

(1)   (2)   (3)

6   6   5   6   3   5

False.
(*See next frame.*)

4.5   Each of the examples in the preceding frame demonstrates

similar motion (True/False) _____.

---

(4).

4.6   In the first example of Frame 4.4 the voices move in the
same direction *by the same interval*. In similar motion the voices
do not move by the same interval.
    Which of the examples below demonstrates similar

motion? _____

(1)   (2)   (3)   (4)

4.7   Compare the two examples below:

(1)   (2)

6   5   6   6

(1) demonstrates *similar* motion (both voices move in the same
direction but not by the same interval). In (2), however, the voices
not only move in the same direction, but also by the same interval.
This is called PARALLEL motion.
    In *parallel* motion the voices not only move in the same

interval

direction, but also by the same _____.

4.8   Write the figured bass symbol for each interval.

(1)   (2)   (3)

—   —   —   —   —   —

parallel

4.9   The examples in the preceding frame show that parallel motion is easily detected by referring to the intervals between the two voices. A succession of like intervals such as 3-3, 5-5 or 6-6 produces

_____motion.

4.10   Write the notes indicated by the figured bass symbols in each case.

(1)   (2)   (3)

5   5   3   3   8   8

parallel

4.11   Each of the examples in the preceding frame demonstrates

_____motion.

(2).

4.12   Which of the examples below demonstrates *parallel*

motion? _____

(1)   (2)   (3)   (4)

(4).

4.13   Which of the examples in the preceding frame

demonstrates *similar* motion? _____

4.14   Compare the two examples below:

Both (1) and (2) demonstrate parallel motion, yet there *is* a difference: in (1) a minor sixth is followed by a major sixth, whereas both intervals are minor sixths in (2).

From this you can see that the term *parallel motion* does not always refer to absolutely parallel voices. We refer to voices as moving in parallel motion when the basic intervals are the same (third to third or sixth to sixth, etc.) without consideration of the specific quality of each interval.

Both (1) and (2) are examples of parallel motion; but (2), illogically, is "more parallel" than (1).

The term parallel motion does not usually take into account

the precise quality of the _____.

intervals

4.15   When it is necessary to identify absolutely parallel motion, phrases such as "parallel major thirds," "perfect fifths," or "minor sixths" may be used.

Some parellel intervals are forbidden in traditional writing. These are parallel perfect unisons, perfect fifths and perfect octaves.

Perfect unisons, perfect fifths and perfect octaves are such pure consonances that voices moving parallel by these intervals tend to lose their individuality.

List the intervals which should not occur in parallel motion:

(1) _____

(2) _____

(3) _____

(1)   Perfect unison

(2)   Perfect fifth

(3)   Perfect octave   *(Any order.)*

(4).	4.16 Which examples illustrates incorrect parallel motion? (*Look for consecutive perfect unisons, fifths, or octaves.*) _____
(2).	4.17 Which example illustrates incorrect parallel motion? _____
(3). *(Example (5) is NOT incorrect because there is no motion, i.e., no change of pitch in either note.)*	4.18 Which example illustrates incorrect parallel motion? _____
No. *(Both (2) and (3) are diminished fifths.)*	4.19 Are all of the intervals in the example below perfect fifths? _____
No. *(The second interval is a diminished fifth.)*	4.20 Parallel fifths are incorrect only if both are *perfect*. Does the example below illustrate incorrect use of parallel motion? _____

(4)

4.21   The preceding frame demonstrates that parallel fifths are incorrect only if both are *perfect*.
 Which of the examples below illustrates *incorrect* parallel

motion? _____

(1)   (2)   (3)   (4)

---

(2), (5)
(Note in example (5) that incorrect parallel motion cannot be corrected by a substitution of the same pitch in a different octave, let alone the spacing problem created.)

4.22   Which of the examples below illustrates *incorrect* parallel

motion?_____

(1)   (2).   (3)   (4)   (5)

---

(3).

4.23   In which case is the parallel motion *correct*?_____

(1)   (2)   (3)   (4)

Your answer is probably *No*. These consecutive intervals are forbidden not because they are offensive, but because they reduce the independence of the voices.

4.24   Perfect unisons, fifths and octaves which appear consecutively between any two voices in four-part writing are forbidden because they tend to destroy temporarily the independence of one of the voices. Consecutive perfect intervals have long been one of the chief stumbling blocks for students of harmony. You should be able to avoid this problem. Instructions will be given later (Frame 4.79) which will help you detect paralled intervals in a four-part texture.
 You may wonder why we must avoid consecutive intervals which, in themselves, do not sound unpleasant. Much music does, in fact, make extensive use of these intervals. (see NOTE.) This study, however, is devoted to tonal harmony as practiced by composers of the baroque, classical and romantic eras. The works of these composers clearly reveal the desire to preserve the integrity of individual voices—an integrity which consecutive perfect intervals tend to destroy.
 Play a succession of paralled perfect fifths at the piano. Do you

think they produce an offensive effect? _____

NOTE: Parallel triads as well as seventh and ninth chords occur frequently in the music of the impressionist composers Debussy and Ravel. Melodic doubling at all intervals is a prominent feature in much twentieth-century music.

Both √

4.25   Check (√) the correct option:

1. In both similar and parallel motion the voices move in the same direction.

2. In parallel motion the voices move in the same direction and by the same basic interval.

True statements:

(1) _____ (2) _____ Both _____ Neither _____

---

(2).

4.26   OBLIQUE motion is demonstrated in the example below:

(1)   (2)

In *oblique* motion one voice is stationary while the second voice moves to another pitch (either upward or downward).
Which of the examples below demonstrates *oblique* motion? ____

(1)   (2)   (3)   (4)

---

(4).

4.27   Which of the examples below demonstrates *oblique* motion?

_____

(1)   (2)   (3)   (4)

4.28   Write the notes indicated by the figured bass symbols.

(1)   (2)   (3)

5   3   6   5   6   3

oblique

4.29   Each of the examples in the preceding frame demonstrates

_____motion.

4.30   CONTRARY motion is demonstrated in the example below:

(1)   (2)   (3)   (4)

Two voices which move in *opposite directions* produce

_____ motion.

contrary

4.31   Write the notes indicated by the figured bass symbols.

(1)   (2)   (3)

3   5   8   3   5   8

(3).

(1)   (2)   (3)

3   5   8   3   5   8

4.32   Each of the examples in the preceding frame demonstrates contrary motion. In which example below does contrary motion

occur? _____

(1)   (2)   (3)   (4)

4.33   List the type of motion in each example.

(1) _____

(2) _____

(3) _____

(4) _____

(1)   Oblique

(2)   Parallel

(3)   Contrary

(4)   Similar

4.34   List the type of motion is each example.

(1) _____

(2) _____

(3) _____

(4) _____

(1)   Contrary

(2)   Similar

(3)   Parallel

(4)   Oblique

(No response)

4.35   The four types of relative motion (parallel, similar, oblique and contrary) result in varying degrees of dependence and independence between the voices concerned. In most cases it is desirable to achieve a balance between these types of motion. Music in which any one type predominates noticeably over the others lacks variety in this important respect. It is important that you continue to take note of the way voices relate to one another as you proceed with this study.

4.36   VOICE LEADING concerns the *horizontal* aspect of harmony and is no less important than the *vertical* aspect (doubling and spacing). The voices, which when sounding together produce chords, must be conceived as melodic lines, and care taken that each leads smoothly from one chord to the next. Although leaps are often desirable, the "smoothest" voice leading results when the voices proceed largely by step.

To demonstrate the characteristics of good voice leading we shall analyze the melodic interval used in a chorale phrase harmonized by

J. S. Bach. You are to scan each of the voices separately and count the number of times a tone is followed by the same tone (repetition), the number of times seconds occur, and the number of times leaps of a third occur. Complete the tabulations and indicate the total for each category.

(The soprano has been analyzed as an example.)

Bach, Chorale: *Befiel du deine Wege*

	Rep.	2nd	3rd
S:	0	8	0
A:	2	7	0
T:	2	6	1
B:	2	8	1
T:	6	29	2

	Repetition	2nd	3rd
SOPRANO:	0	8	0
ALTO:			
TENOR:			
BASS:			
TOTAL:			

4.37   Of the total melodic intervals in the preceding example 78% are major or minor seconds. Not all music displays such notable smoothness of voice leading. Indeed, melodic leaps of a fourth or more occasionally are used for their expressive value. The example above does serve, however, to demonstrate the smoothness which results when step-wise motion predominates.

You should strive for smooth voice leading. This is accom-

step

plished by having a predominance of _____-wise motion.

4.38   All augmented intervals, but especially the augmented second and the augmented fourth, should be avoided as melodic intervals when writing vocal music. These intervals are awkward to sing and composers of the baroque and classical eras took pains to avoid their use.

Which of the examples below is incorrect (in terms of the above statement)? _____

(4).

augmented second	4.39 What interval is demonstrated in (4) of the preceding frame? The _____ _____.
(3).	4.40 Which example demonstrates awkward melodic movement? _____
augmented second	4.41 What interval is demonstrated in (3) of the preceding frame The _____ _____.
(2).	4.42 Which example demonstrates awkward melodic movement?_____
augmented fourth	4.43 What interval is demonstrated in (2) of the precediung frame? The _____ _____.
(1) M2 (2) A2 (3) P4 (4) A4	4.44 Name the melodic interval of each example (use abbreviations). _____ _____ _____ _____
(2) A2; (4) A4.	4.45 Which of the examples in the preceding frame demonstrate intervals which should be avoided when writing vocal music? _____

(No response)

4.46   The augmented second and the augmented fourth sometimes occur as melodic intervals in instrumental music. This is due to the fact that instrumentalists do not have the problem of finding their pitch as do vocalists. Even in instrumental music, however, these intervals often are avoided for the sake of smooth melodic writing. In addition, instrumental music of the eighteenth and early nineteenth centuries was strongly influencd by vocal music. Thus it is natural that vocal melodic concepts should be reflected in instrumental styles.

   Melodic intervals of the augmented second and the augmented fourth are not absolutely prohibited, but they should be avoided, particularly in music intended for voices.

4.47   An augmented second is used as a melodic interval in the example below. Find this interval and indicate it with the sign (⌐‾x2‾¬).

Bach, *Well-Tempered Clavier*, Vol. 1, Prelude XII
(Andante)

4.48   An augmented fourth appears in the example below. Find this interval and indicate it with the sign (⌐‾x4‾¬).

Beethoven, *Sonatina in F Major*
Allegro assai

4.49   The remainder of this chapter is devoted to the mechanics of voice leading. Before proceeding. however, let us review the principles upon which this study will be based.

   The two chief concerns of part writing are the doubling and spacing of triad tones to produce agreeable sonorities, and leading the voices smoothly from one chord to another so that each voice constitutes an expressive melodic line.

Keep in mind the following principles regarding the part writing of triads in root position:

DOUBLING:
1.   When a triad is in root position the bass is generally doubled.
2.   Each chord should contain two roots, one third and one fifth.
SPACING:
3.   The voices should be in normal distribution (from upper to lower: soprano, alto, tenor and bass).
4.   The interval between adjacent upper voices should not exdeed an octave.
VOICE LEADING:
5.   Step-wise motion should predominate in leading voices from one chord to another.
6.   Melodic leaps of a augmented interval, but especially the augmented second or augmented fourth, should be avoided.
7.   Consecutive perfect unisons, fifths, or octaves are forbidden.

(No response.)

4.50   When a chord in root position is repeated it is often desirable to change the position of some (or all) of the upper voices. In the example below, the static effect of (1) is avoided in (2) by moving each of the upper voices down one triad tone; in (3) the root and third have been exchanged in the sporano and tenor voices. Thus, for repeated root position chords, try to retain the common tones whenever possible and move the remaining tones to the nearest chord tones to achieve correct doubling and spacing.

Which triad tone is doubled in each chord above? The (root/3rd/ 5th) _____

root

4.51   Notice that in (3) of the preceding frame there is a change from close to open structure, whereas in (2) both chords are in close structure. Change of structure occurs frequently upon chord repetition.

Write the alto and tenor voices for the second chord in each case *without change of structure.*

(If your solutions do not agree with the answers given check the doubling and spacing.)

4.52   Write the alto and tenor voices for the second chord in each case *without change of structure.*

(Continue to check your solutions as in the preceding frame.)

4.53   Write the alto and tenor voices for the second chord in each case. *Change structure on the second chord.*

(Before looking at the answers, check: have you changed structure on the second chord?)

4.54   Write the alto and tenor voices for the second chord in each case. *Change structure on the second chord.*

(Have you changed structure on the second chord?)

Incorrect doubling.
(*There is no fifth in the second chord.*)

4.55   What is the part writing error in the example below?

_____

In the second chord the interval between the alto and tenor is greater than an octave. (*Or equivalent.*)

4.56   What is the part writing error in the example below?

_____

4.47   In a succession of two chords there are often tones which occur in both. These are called COMMON TONES. When a triad is repeated both chords obviously contain the same tones.

Triad tones:
{ G - G
  E - E
  C - C }

three | The two chords above have _____ common tones.

4.58   The part writing of triads which have the same root is relatively simple — the chief concern is with redistributing the tones to produce correct doubling and spacing.

EGB. | Name the common tones in the chords below: _____

4.59   Whereas there are *three* common tones when a chord is repeated, there is only one common tone between triads whose roots are a fifth apart*

Triad tones:
{ G   D   G   C
  E   B   E   A
  C   G   C   F }

In both of these examples the common tone has been retained in the same voice. In (1) the common tone is in the tenor; in (2) it

soprano | is in the _____.

*Root movement a fifth upward is the same as a fourth downward and vice versa. Statements regarding root movement by fifths apply equally to root movement by fourths.

	4.60 The examples in the preceding frame demonstrate the first method of part writing triads whose roots are a fifth apart. Learn this:
	PRINCIPLE 1
	When connecting triads whose roots are a fifth (or fourth) apart, retain the common tone in the same voice and move the remaining voices to the NEAREST chord tones to achieve correct doubling and spacing.
	How many tones are common to two triads whose roots are a fifth
One	apart? _____
D.	4.61 Name the tone which is common to the triads below: _____
Yes. *(D has been retained in the tenor.)*	4.62 Has the common tone been retained in the same voice in the preceding frame?_____ .
	4.63 Write the alto and tenor voices for the second chord in each case. *Retain the common tone in the same voice.*

4.64   Write the alto and tenor voices for the second chord in each case. *Retain the common tone in the same voice.*

4.65   Write the alto and tenor voices for the second chord in each case. *Retain the common tone in the same voice.*

4.66   Notice in (3) of the preceding frame that the tenor was forced to leap a fourth to find a triad tone which resulted in correct doubling and spacing. *This is satisfactory.* Such leaps, however, must not occur too frequently, and should enhance the expressiveness of the melodic lines.

    Write the alto and tenor voices for the second chord in each case. *Retain the common tone in the same voice.*

4.67   Examine the example below:

The common tone in this example is G. Has this tone

been retained in the same voice?_____

No.

4.68   The preceding example demonstrates the second method of part writing triads whose roots are a fifth apart.   Learn this:

EXCEPTION 1

If, when connecting triads whose roots are a fifth (or fourth) apart the common tone is NOT retained in the same voice, move all voices to the NEAREST chord tones which result in correct doubling and spacing.

In the example of the preceding frame the common tone (G) occurs in the alto of the first chord. In the second chord this tone is in

the _____.

tenor

4.69   The key word in the Exception stated in the preceding frame is "nearest." It is seldom necessary to leap more than a third in any of the upper voices. Any leap larger than a third should be examined carefully; it may be symptomatic of a part writing error.

Write the alto and tenor voices for the second chord in each case. *Do NOT retain the common tone in the same voice.*

(1)   (2)   (3)   (1)   (2)   (3)

4.70   Write the alto and tenor voices for the second chord in each case. *Do NOT retain the common tone in the same voice.*

4.71   Write the alto and tenor voices for the second chord in each case. *Do NOT retain the common tone in the same voice.*

4.72   Write the alto and tenor voices and supply the Roman numeral analysis. *Use CLOSE structure for all chords.*

4.73   Write the alto and tenor voices and supply the Roman numeral analysis. *Use OPEN structure for all chords.*

4.74   Write the alto and tenor voices and supply the Roman numeral analysis. *Use OPEN structure for all chords.*

a: __ __ __ __ __

4.75   There are NO common tones between triads whose roots are a second apart. List the triad tone for each of the chords below:

Triad tones: __ __

F   G
A   B
C   D

No.
(*There are no common tones.*)

4.76   Learn this:

PRINCIPLE II

When connecting triads whose roots are a second apart, move all the upper voices to the nearest chord tones in CONTRARY MOTION to the bass.

Can a common tone be retained when connecting triads whose roots are a second apart? _____

4.77   Write the soprano, alto and tenor voices for the second chord in each case. Be sure that all of the upper voices move to their nearest chord tone in *contrary motion* to the bass.

(1)   (2)   (3)

(1)   (2)   (3)

4.78 Write the soprano, alto and tenor voices for the second chord in each case. Be sure that all of the upper voices move to their nearest chord tone in *contrary motion* to the bass.

4.79 If you fail to move the upper voices in contrary motion to the bass (when connecting triads whose roots are a second apart) parallel fifths and octaves are likely to occur. In all future work you should check for incorrect use of parallel motion each time you part write a chord. *Be especially alert when the bass moves a second.*

To be certain you have not written consecutive perfect intervals you should check the motion between each of the voices as follows:

1.   From the bass to each of the upper voices.
2.   From the tenor to the alto and soprano.
3.   From the alto to the soprano.

Incorrect parallel motion is more likely to occur when the bass moves a (5th/2nd) _____.

2nd

4.80 Apply the method described in the preceding frame by tabulating the intervals between the various voices for each of the chords below (the first has been done as an example):

	1st	2nd
(1)	M3	m3
(2)	P5	P5
(3)	P8	P8
(4)	m3	M3
(5)	m6	M6
(6)	P4	P4

		1st Chord M3	2nd Chord m3
(1)	Bass and Tenor	M3	m3
(2)	Bass and Alto	_____	_____
(3)	Bass and Soprano	_____	_____
(4)	Tenor and Alto	_____	_____
(5)	Tenor and Soprano	_____	_____
(6)	Alto and Soprano	_____	_____

bass (and) alto

4.81   In a check such as that of the preceding frame incorrect parallel motion shows up as a succession of perfect unisons, fifths or octaves *between the same two voices*. In this case incorrect parallel motion occurs not only between the bass and soprano, but also between the _____ and _____.

4.82   For additional practice in detecting incorrect parallel motion tabulate the intervals between the various voices in each of the chords below:

(*Note: The first chord is not in root position.*)

	1st	2nd
(1)	m3	M3
(2)	m6	P8
(3)	m3	P5
(4)	P4	m6
(5)	P8	m3
(6)	P5	P5

		1st Chord	2nd Chord
(1)	Bass and Tenor	_____	_____
(2)	Bass and Alto	_____	_____
(3)	Bass and Soprano	_____	_____
(4)	Tenor and Alto	_____	_____
(5)	Tenor and Soprano	_____	_____
(6)	Alto and Soprano	_____	_____

---

alto (and) soprano

4.83   Between which voices does incorrect parallel motion occur in the preceding frame? Between the _____ and _____.

---

bass (and) alto

4.84   The method of checking for incorrect parallel motion described in Frame 4.79 seems at first to be laborious. There is no other way, however, to be certain that you have made no mistakes and you will soon find ways to speed the process. By using this method each time you part write a chord, many careless mistakes will be avoided.

Between which voices does incorrect parallel motion occur in the example on the next page? Between the _____ and _____.

F: I   I   IV   V   I

4.85   Write the alto and tenor voices and supply the Roman numeral analysis. *Use CLOSE structrue for all chords.*

F: ___   ___   ___   ___   ___

e: i   iv   V   V   i

4.86   Write the alto and tenor voices and supply the Roman numeral analysis. *Use OPEN structure for all chords.*

e: ___   ___   ___   ___   ___

4.87   Examine the progression below:

The bass has not been doubled.
(There are two 3rds instead of two roots.)

What irregularity occurs in the second chord?_____

_____

4.88   The preceding frame demonstrates an exception to the usual method of part writing triads whose roots are a second apart. Learn this:

EXCEPTION 2
*When the bass moves UP a second, one voice may move in parallel thirds (or tenths) with the bass, resulting in a double third in the second chord.**

Except for the voice which moves in parallel thirds (or tenths) with the bass, all upper voices move normally (down in

contrary

_____motion to the bass).

_____

*Exception 2 does apply to the progression IV-V, where it would result in a doubled leading tone (See Frames 5.91 and 5.98.)

4.89   Which of the examples below demonstrates the Exception stated in the preceding frame? (*Look for a double third in the second*

(3).

*chord.)*_____

4.90   Note in (3) of the preceding frame that all of the upper voices move normally (in contrary motion to the bass) except the one which moves up in parallel tenths.
   Write the soprano, alto and tenor voices for the second chord applying the exception stated in Frame 4.88. (*Remember: the third must be doubled in the second chord.*)

4.91   Continue as in the preceding frame.

4.92   The irregularity of doubling described in Frame 4.88 is used most often as a means of avoiding the augmented second which otherwise occurs when progressing from V to VI in harmonic minor.

   If all voices move in contrary motion to the bass an augmented second results as is shown in (1). The usual solution to this problem is shown in (2). The irregular doubling in the second example is less offensive than the augmented second in the first.

   When progressing from V to VI in harmonic minor, the second

chord will usually contain a double _____.

third

4.93   Write the alto and tenor voices and supply the Roman numeral analysis. *(Irregular doubling must occur in the final chord.)*

a: i   iv   i   V   VI

4.94   Write the alto and tenor voices and supply the Roman numerals analysis.

g: ___   ___   ___   ___   ___

4.95   There are *two* common tones between triads whose roots are a third apart.

Triad tones: G ——— E   G ——— B
               E ——— C   E ——— G
               C ——— A   C ——— E

The above example demonstrates the usual method of part writing triads whose roots are a third apart.   Learn this:

PRINCIPLE 3

When connecting triads whose roots are a third apart, retain two common tones and move the remaining voice to the nearest chord tone.

In applying the principle stated above, how many of

the upper voices will move? _____

One.

4.96   Write the soprano, alto and tenor voices for the second chord in each case. *Retain TWO common tones in the same voices.*

4.97   Write the soprano, alto and tenor voices for the second chord in each case. *Retain TWO common tones in the same voices.*

4.98   Write the alto and tenor voices and supply the Roman numeral analysis.

F: I   vi   IV   V   I

F: ___   ___   ___   ___   ___

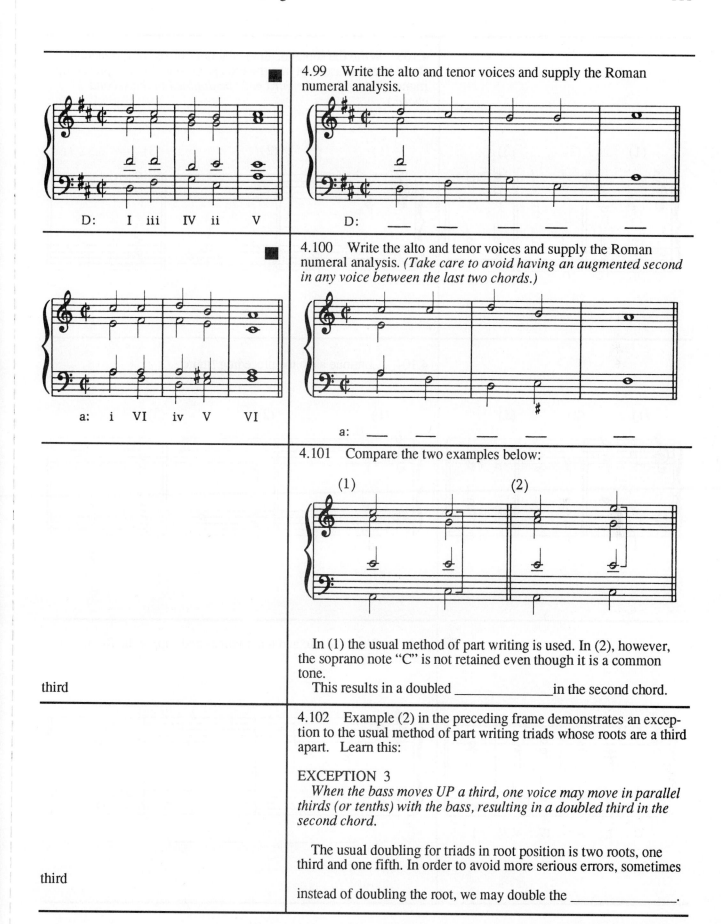

4.99 Write the alto and tenor voices and supply the Roman numeral analysis.

D: ___ ___ ___ ___ ___

D: I iii IV ii V

4.100 Write the alto and tenor voices and supply the Roman numeral analysis. *(Take care to avoid having an augmented second in any voice between the last two chords.)*

a: ___ ___ ___ ___ ___

a: i VI iv V VI

4.101 Compare the two examples below:

(1)   (2)

In (1) the usual method of part writing is used. In (2), however, the soprano note "C" is not retained even though it is a common tone.

This results in a doubled _____ in the second chord.

third

4.102 Example (2) in the preceding frame demonstrates an exception to the usual method of part writing triads whose roots are a third apart. Learn this:

EXCEPTION 3
When the bass moves UP a third, one voice may move in parallel thirds (or tenths) with the bass, resulting in a doubled third in the second chord.

The usual doubling for triads in root position is two roots, one third and one fifth. In order to avoid more serious errors, sometimes

instead of doubling the root, we may double the _____.

third

4.103 Write the soprano, alto and tenor voices for the second chord in each case applying the Exception stated in the preceding frame. (*Remember: the third must be doubled in the second chord.*)

4.104 Continue as in the preceding frame.

4.105 Write the alto and tenor voices and supply the Roman numeral analysis.

C: I   I   IV   V   I

C: __   __   __   __   __

4.106 Write the alto and tenor voices and supply the Roman numeral analysis. (*Be alert when part writing the last two chords.*)

e: i   VI   iv   V   VI

e: ___ ___ ___ ___

4.107 Irregular doubling should not occur in several chords in sucession. Return immediately to normal doubling after a chord in which irregular doubling occurs.

Write the alto and tenor voices and supply the Roman numeral analysis. Irregular doubling will occur at the asterisk. Take care that the doubled tones are left in *contrary* motion.

G: I   iii   ii   V   I

G: ___ ___ ___ ___ ___

4.108 Write the alto and tenor voices and supply the Roman numeral analysis. Irregular doubling will occur at the asteriak. Return to normal doubling immediately.

A: I   iii   IV   vi   V

A: ___ ___ ___ ___ ___

Summary

Part writing is not an exact science. No absolute rules can be established to guarantee good musical effects. As we progress further into this study it will become increasingly necessary to allow your musical instincts to influence your decisions. Principles governing doubling, spacing and voice leading have been established, but all of these are tempered by practical necessities. The nearest thing to a "rule" is the prohibition against parallel perfect unisons, fifths and octaves. For the present, these should be avoided, even at the expense of normal doubling, spacing or voice leading.

The most important principle: The smoothest voice leading results if voices always move to the nearest possible chord tones. Retain common tones in the same voice(s) when possible. Leaps in any of the upper voices beyond the nearest chord tones should be carefully scrutinized. You must be able to justify such leaps as being necessary to avoid more serious flaws such as undesirable melodic intervals (augmented seconds and fourths), or parallel unisons, fifths or octaves. Of course leaps sometimes contribute to more effective melodic lines, or are necessary to produce desirable doublings. But for now you should use mostly seconds and thirds — and occasionally fourths — as melodic intervals in the sporano, alto and tenor voices. More frequent use of larger intervals is to be expected in the bass.

These principles should be generally followed for the doubling of triads in root position:

PRINCIPLE 1:   When connecting triads whose roots are a fifth (or fourth) apart, retain the common tone in the same voice and move the remaining voices to the nearest chord tones to achieve correct doubling and spacing.

EXCEPTION 1:   If, when connecting triads whose roots are a fifth (or fourth) apart the common tone is *not* retained in the same voice, move all voices to the *nearest* chord tones that result in correct doubling and spacing.

PRINCIPLE 2:   When connecting triads whose roots are a second apart, move all the upper voices to the nearest chord tones in *contrary motion* to the bass.

EXCEPTION 2:   When the bass moves *up* a second, one voice may move in parallel thirds (or tenths) with the bass, resulting in a doubled third in the second chord.

PRINCIPLE 3:   When connecting triads whose roots are a third apart, retain two common tones and move the remaining voice to the nearest chord tone.

EXCEPTION 3:   When the bass moves *up* a third, one voice may move in parallel thirds (or tenths) with the bass, resulting in a doubled third in the second chord.

Mastery Frames

4–1   Identify the type of relative motion in each example below.

(1)   (2)   (3)   (4)

(1)   Parallel

(2)   Similar

(3)   Oblique

(4)   Contrary

(4.1–.14, 4.26–.34)

Parallel perfect fifths normally are forbidden.
(4.15–.24)

4–2   Why is the motion in Example (1) in the previous frame incorrect?
_____

_____

4–3   Write the alto and tenor voices and provide the Roman numeral analysis. *Use close structure.*

(1)   (2)   (3)

a: i   iv   G: ii   V   d: V   i

(1)   (2)   (3)

a: __   __   G: __   __   d: __   __

(4.59–.74)

---

(3).
(4.59–.62)

4–4   In which example in Frame 4–1 has the common tone been retained in the same voice? _____

(1)   **(2)**   **(3)**

C: I   vi   F: I   iii   g: VI   iv

(4.75–.94)

To avoid an A 2nd in the tenor voice.

(4.92)

4–5   Write the alto and tenor voices and provide the Roman numeral analysis. *Use open structure.*

(1) Open   **(2) Close**   **(3) Close**

C: __ __   F: __ __   g: __ __

4–6   Explain why it was necessary to double the third in the final chord in Example (3) of Frame 4-5.

_____

_____

_____

---

(1)   **(2)**   **(3)**

D: I   ii   Bb: V   vi   a: V   VI

(4.95–.108)

4–7   Write the alto and tenor voices and provide the Roman numeral analysis. *Use the structure indicated.*

(1)   **(2)**   **(3)**

D: __ __   Bb: __ __   a: __ __

Supplementary Assignments

ASSIGNMENT 4–1   Name _____

1.   Write an example in two voices of each type of relative motion as indicated.

2.   Which examples show *incorrect* parallel motion? _____

3.   Which examples show *incorrect* parallel motion? _____

4.   Which type of relative motion results in the greatest independence between two voices? _____

(1)   Similar

(2)   Parallel

(3)   Contrary

(4)   Oblique

5. Name the two intervals which should be avoided in melodic writing.

      1. _____   2._____

6. Name the undesirable interval which occurs in the example below.

     e:

7. Select the preferred version. _____

    C: I   -   -   -   -   -   -   -

8. Select the preferred version. _____

    e: V   i   V   i   V   i   V   i

9. Select the preferred version._____

    Bb: IV   V   IV   V   IV   V   IV   V

ASSIGNMENT 4–2   Name _____

1.   Write the alto and tenor voices. (*Observe the rules of doubling and spacing.*)

b: V   VI   Eb: I   iii   G: I   I   d: iv   i

2.   Write the alto and tenor voices. (*Observe the rules of doubling and spacing.*)

C: I   vi   f#:   i   V   c: i   i   F: IV   V

3.   Choose one or more of the options below for each example.

(A) _____ (B) _____ (C) _____

G: a: C:

(1)   Incorrect doubling

(2)   Incorrect spacing

(3)   Incorrect melodic interval

(4)   Incorrect parallel motion

(5)   No error

4. Choose one or more of the options below for each example.

(A) _____ (B) _____ (C) _____

(1) Incorrect doubling   (4) Figured bass not realized

(2) Incorrect spacing   (5) No error under the circumstances

(3) Incorrect parallel motion

5. Write the alto and tenor voices and analyze with Roman numerals.

Chapter 5.0
Triads in First and Second Inversion

Depending upon whether the root, third, or fifth is in the bass, triads are said to be in: root position, first inversion, or second inversion. Inversions are used to produce a variety of chordal effects and enhance the melodic character of the bass line. The principles which govern the part writing of triads in first and second inversion are presented in this chapter.

lowest *(or bass)*	5.1 A triad is in *root position* when the lowest tone is the root. If the tones of a triad are arranged so that the root is not in the lowest voice, the triad is INVERTED. A triad is inverted by placing the third or fifth in the _____voice.
second	5.2 Compare the three chords below: If the third of a triad is in the bass, the triad is in first inversion; if the fifth of a triad is in the bass, the triad is in _____inversion.
D.	5.3 If the B-flat major triad is in first inversion, what is the lowest note? _____
C-sharp	5.4 If the F-sharp minor triad is in the second inversion, what is the lowest note? _____

G.	5.5 If the G major triad is in root position, what is the lowest note?_____
A.	5.6 If the D minor triad is in second inversion, what is the lowest note?_____
A-flat.	5.7 If the F diminished triad is in first inversion, what is the lowest note?_____
bass (or lowest)	5.8 It is important to know which tone is the root of each chord. This is no problem when all chords are in root position. But when some of the chords are inverted, you must rearrange the tones mentally in order to locate the root. In progressions which include inversions, the root will not always be in the _____voice.
first (or) second	5.9 When analyzing a chord which may or may not be an inversion it is a good idea to notice first if the notes can be arranged in thirds above the bass. This is because many triads are in root position. If the notes of a triad *cannot* be arranged in thirds above the bass it means that the triad is in either _____ or _____ inversion.
	5.10 To find the root of an inverted triad you must mentally rearrange the notes to produce a succession of thirds. The root, of course, will be the lowest note when they are arranged in this manner. Try each successive note until you find the one upon which thirds can be built. We shall demonstrate this process. Notice in the example below that the notes arranged above the bass as in (a) are CEA. The interval E to A is a fourth, so C is not the root. Arranged above the tenor as in (b), however, the notes are ACE. The notes now are arranged in thirds, so the lowest note (A) is the root.

thirds

(1) F

(2) G

(3) E

(4) C♯

(1) F

(2) B

(3) A♭

(4) D

(1) E♭

(2) G♯

(3) F♯

(4) G

The root of a triad is always the lowest note when the notes are arranged in _____.

5.11 Indicate the *root* of each chord.

Root: ___   ___   ___   ___

5.12 Indicate the *root* of each chord.

Root: ___   ___   ___   ___

5.13 Indicate the *root* of each chord.

Root: ___   ___   ___   ___

5.14   The root, third or fifth of a triad may appear in the bass. The same may be said of the soprano. The result is nine possible positions of any triad (with reference to the bass and soprano only).

THE G MAJOR TRIAD (in four voices.)

(Play the nine positions of the G major triad as illustrated above. Listen to the different sonority of each position.)

All triads in root position sound alike. (True/False) _____

False
(The note in the soprano and the spacing of the notes affect the sound of a triad.)

5.15   A triad in *first inversion* has the intervals of a sixth and a third above the lowest note.

The figured bass symbol ₆₃ indicates a triad in

_____ inversion.

first

5.16   The number 6 is sufficient to indicate a triad (chord) in first inversion. The complete figuration ₆₃ is used only if needed to show alterations.

(1)   (2)   (3)

In the example above, merely the number 6 is adequate in (1) as neither the third nor the sixth is altered; in (2) the A-sharp is shown by the slash through the 6; a sharp is added to the figured bass in (3) to show the alteration of E to E-sharp.

3rd	The number 6 in the figured bass means that the note in the bass is the (root/3rd/5th) _____ of the chord.

	5.17 Spell the root position **triad** implied by each of the figured bass symbols.
(1) EGB	(1) (2) (3)
(2) G♯ BD	
(3) ACE♭	6 ⌀6 6♭
	(1) _____ (2) _____ (3) _____

	5.18 Spell the root position **triad** implied by each of the figured bass symbols.
(1) BDF♯	(1) (2) (3)
(2) DFA	
(3) B♭DF	6♯ 6 ♭6
	(1) _____ (2) _____ (3) _____

	5.19 Spell the root position **triad** implied by each of the figured bass symbols.
(1) E♯ G♯ B♯	(1) (2) (3)
(2) DF♯ A♯	
(3) A♭ CE ♭	⌀6♯ 6♯ ♭6♭
	(1) _____ (2) _____ (3) _____

	5.20 Check (√) the correct option:
	1. The figured bass symbol "6" represents a triad in first inversion.
	2. The figured bass symbol "6" means that the bass note is the root of the triad.
	True statements:
(1) √	(1) _____ (2) _____ Both _____ Neither _____

5.21 A triad in *second inversion* has intervals of a sixth and fourth above the lowest note.

A triad in second inversion is indicated by the figured bass symbol $\frac{6}{4}$. In second inversion the tone in the bass is the (root/3rd/5th) _____ of the triad.

5th

5.22 Neither the 6 or the 4 can be omitted from the figured bass in the case of a triad in second inversion.

Notice that in (1) both the number 6 and the number 4 are used even though the notes represented by these numbers are not altered.

Write the figured bass symbol which indicates a triad in second inversion. _____

$\frac{6}{4}$.

5.23 Spell the root position triad implied by each of the figured bass symbols.

(1) F♯AC♯

(2) CEG

(3) B♭DF

(1) _____   (2) _____   (3) _____

5.24   Spell the root position triad implied by each of the figured bass symbols.

(1)   EG♯B

(2)   A♭ C♭ E♭

(3)   GBD

(1) _____ (2) _____ (3) _____

5.25   Spell the root position triad inplied by each of the figured bass symbols.

(1)   G♯ B♯ D♯

(2)   BD♯F

(3)   G♭ B♭ D♭

(1) _____ (2) _____ (3) _____

5.26   Write the notes on the staff indicated by the figured bass symbols.

5.27   Continue as in the preceding frame.

5.28 Continue as in the preceding frame.

(2)
(There are fewer and smaller leaps.)

Which of these examples has the "smoother" bass line?_____

5.30 The use of inversions permits the bass line to flow more smoothly, thereby producing a better melodic line. This is an important reason for using inversions.

inversions.

A more melodic bass line results from the use of _____

5.31 Play again the two examples of Frame 5.29. As all of the chords of (1) are in root position, there is a uniformity of sonority. The contrast in sonority provided by inversions in (2) adds greatly to the musical interest. This is the second reason for using inversions.

   Inversions contribute to the musical interest in two ways: the bass line may become more melodic, and there can be a greater variety of sonorities.

(No response.)

	5.32 The character of triads varies according to whether they are in root position, first inversion, or second inversion. You must become sensitive to these differences through listening experiences. Major and minor triads in root position provide the most stable sonorities. Triads in first inversion, however, are less stable; they help motivate the harmony by demanding resolution into more stable sonorities. A sense of "forward motion" is imparted by the use of first inversions.
(No response.)	Triads in second inverson are still less stable than those in first inversion. Because of the relatively weak sonority of triads in second inversion, they are used sparingly.
	5.33 First and second inversions are shown when analyzing with Roman numerals by including the appropriate figured bass symbol as part of the chord symbol.
second	The number $\begin{smallmatrix}6\\4\end{smallmatrix}$ added to a Roman numeral indicate that the chord is in _____inversion.
3rd	5.34 The chord symbol I^6 indicates that the (root/3rd/5th) _____of the tonic triad is in the bass.
(1) A: I^6 (2) d: iv^6 (3) c: V	5.35 Write the appropriate chord symbol in each case. *(Be sure to show the inversion.)*

5.36   Continue as in the preceding frame.

e: ____   D: ____   B♭: ____

(1)   e: iv$^6_4$

(2)   D: vii^{o6}

(3)   B♭:   ii^6

5.37   Continue as in the preceding frame.

C: ____   f♯: ____   g: ____

(1)   C: I$^6_4$

(2)   f♯:   V^6

(3)   g: i

5.38   We shall now turn our attention to part writing triads in first inversion.   Learn this:

PRINCIPLE 4

When a major or minor triad is in first inversion, the soprano is usually doubled.

6   6   6

When a triad is in root position, the bass is usually doubled. The voice which is doubled when a triad is in first inversion

is usually the_____.

soprano

5.39

Write the alto and tenor voices for each chord. *(Be sure the soprano is doubled.)*

5.40   Continue as in the preceding frame.

5.41   Continue as in the preceding frame.

(1) **(2)**

or   or

---

(3).
(There is more than an octave between the alto and tenor voices.)

---

(1) √

5.42 Continue as in the preceding frame.

(1) **(2)**

6   6
#

5.43 The preceding four frames have shown that first inversions often give rise to several possibilities of spacing. Take care that the interval between adjacent upper voices is not larger than an octave, and do not use notes which are outside the normal range of each voice. (See Frame 3.26).

When triads are in first inversion the doubled tone varies. It is the root, third or fifth depending on which of these is in the soprano.

Which of the triads below contains a part writing error? _____

(1) **(2)** **(3)** **(4)**

6   6   ♭6   6

5.44 Considerable freedom is exercised by composers regarding the doubling of triads in first inversion. Doubling usually is determined by the necessity of avoiding a part writing error, or in order to produce a more desirable melodic line in one or more parts. But in spite of this, it is advisable to try the normal doubling *first,* as this usually provides the most satisfactory solution.

Check (√) the correct option:

1. Triads in root position usually have a doubled root.
2. Triads in first inversion usually have a doubled 3rd.

True Statements:

(1) _____ (2) _____ Both _____ Neither _____

5.45   When moving from a triad in first inversion to one in root position, follow the steps outlined below:

1.   Move the doubled tones in contrary, oblique or (rarely) similar motion to the nearest chord tones possible.
2.   Move the remaining voice* to the tone which will complete the triad or which provides correct doubling.

The example below illustrates step one:

The doubled voices have moved to the nearest chord tones

possible in _____motion.
_____
*If the soprano is doubled by the bass, there will be two remaining voices.

contrary

Doubled tones must not be left in parallel motion. *(Or equivalent.)*

5.46   With reference to the example in the preceding frame why is

it undesirable to leave the doubled tones as below? _____

_____

5.47   Step two of the process described in Frame 5.45 is illustrated in (b) below:

The triad tone which was needed to complete the chord was the third (F). The voice which moves to complete the triad (as above) rarely moves more than a second. A larger leap may indicate an error.

Check especially for parallel perfect intervals.

The voice which remains after the doubled voices have found their place in the next chord moves to a tone which completes the

doubling   triad, or which provides correct _____.

5.48   In the example below, perform step one (move the doubled tones in contrary, oblique or similar motion to the nearest chord tones possible).

There is only one correct answer. If your soluion does not agree with the one given, try to find your mistake. Consult your instructor if necessary.

5.49   In the example below, perform step two (move the remaining voice to the tone which will complete the triad or which provides correct doubling).

6

or

5.50   Partwrite the second chord applying the method presented in Frame 5.45.

6

6

or

5.51   Partwrite the second chord.

6

5.52   Partwrite the second chord. Note that, because the soprano is doubled by the bass, *two* voices will remain after the doubled tones have moved. You must fit these remaining voices into the chord in order to achieve correct doubling and spacing.

6

or

6

5.53   Partwrite the second chord.

6

6

5.54   Continue as in the preceding frame

If you chose:

(a)   go to Frame 5.56

(b)   go to Frame 5.57

(c)   go to Frame 5.58

5.55   The first chord below progresses best to ((a), (b) or (c))

_____.

5.56   (a) is a poor choice because the doubled tones in the first chord are left in parallel motion (resulting in parallel octaves between the tenor and soprano). In addition, the doubling of (a) is irregular (there is no fifth).

(No response.)

Return to Frame 5.55 and try again.

5.57   You have selected the best possible solution. By what type of motion have the doubled tones been left? _____

Contrary
(Skip to Frame 5.59.)

5.58   (c) is not the best solution. The leap of a fourth in the soprano (C to F) is unnecessary and the doubling is irregular. Part writing such as this might be used, however, to exploit for expressive purposes the leap in the soprano. This solution is *not* incorrect, but return to Frame 5.55 and find the smoothest possible solution.

(No resopnse.)

soprano

oblique

Contrary.

5.59   When moving from a triad in root position to one in first inversion, follow the steps outlined below:

1.   Move *into* the doubled tones in contrary, oblique, or (rarely) similar motion. *Move all voices by the smallest possible intervals.*

2.   Move the remaining voice(s) to the nearest tone(s) which completes the triad or provides correct doubling.

You will avoid many errors if the doubled tones are written first. The voice which usually is doubled in first inversion triads

is the _____.

5.60   The example below illustrates step one of the process described in the preceding frame:

6

The soprano note is doubled by retaining the common tone in the tenor. Movement into the doubled tones is by

_____motion.

5.61   Step two is illustrated in (b) below:

(a) Step One   (b) Step Two

6   6

The triad tone needed to complete the chord is the fifth (G). The alto is able to move to this tone without producing incorrect parallel motion.

What type of motion occurs between the bass and alto in (b)?

_____

5.62 Write the alto and tenor voices for the second chord in each case, applying the method presented in Frame 5.59

5.63 Continue as in the preceding frame.

5.64 Continue as in the preceding frame.

5.65 Write the alto and tenor voices. *(Use normal doubling in all chords; check carefully for incorrect parallel motion.)*

5.66   Continue as in the preceding frame.

5.67   Continue as in the preceding frame. *(There should be irregular doubling at the asterisk.)*

5.68   What part writing error would have occured in the preceding frame if the tenor had doubled the bass on B-flat in the final chord?

_____

_____

An augmented 2nd used as a
melodic interval. *(Or equivalent.)*

5.69   Write the alto and tenor voices.

5.70   The soprano is usually doubled when major or minor triads are in first inversion. But irregular doubling may occur to avoid incorrect parallel motion or undesirable melodic intervals (particularly the augmented second between V and VI in harmonic minor).

The first step when moving into or out of a first inversion should be to write the voices which are doubled.

(No response.)

5.71   Unlike major and minor triads, the diminished triad is seldom used in either root position or second inversion. This is due to the interval of the diminished fifth which appears between the root and fifth. Compare the three examples below:

In both (1) and (3), the interval of the diminished fifth (or its enharmonic equivalent, the augmented fourth) appears above the *lowest* voice. In (2), however, the diminished fifth appears not above the bass, but above the tenor. In this case the dissonant effect of the diminished fifth is minimized because all the intervals above the bass are consonant (3rd, 6th and octave).

The diminished triad is rarely used in _____ position or

_____ inversion.

root (position or)
second (inversion.)

5.72   Play diminished triads in various positions to see if you agree that the first inversion provides the most agreeable sonority. At any rate, most of the composers of the eighteenth and nineteenth centuries must have thought so, for they used this inversion more frequently than second inversion and especially more so than root position which is the least-used of the three possible positions.
    According to the statements above, which of the following

chords provides the most agreeable sonority? _____

(2).

5.73 Which triad tone is doubled in (2) of the preceding frame?

3rd.

(Root/3rd/5th) _____

5.74 The usual doubling of the diminished triad is illustrated in (2) of Frame 5.72.   Learn this:

EXCEPTION 4

Diminished triads usually are in first inversion with the third (the bass) doubled.

Whereas the soprano is doubled in major and minor triads in first inversion, the diminished triad in first inversion requires that

bass *(or third)*

the_____be doubled.

5.75 Write the alto and tenor for each of the diminished triads below. *(Be sure to double the BASS.)*

5.76 Continue as in the preceding frame.

5.77   Let us review briefly the principles of doubling presented to this point

1.   When a major or minor triad is in *root* position, double the BASS.

2.   When a major or minor triad is in *first inversion*, double the SOPRANO.

3.   Diminished triads should be used in *first inversion* with the BASS (or third) doubled.

(No response.)

(dim. triad)

5.78   Since diminished triads are handled differently from major and minor triads, you must determine the *quality* of each triad before writing.
   Add the alto and tenor voices. *(Remember: It is best to write first the voice which produces the desired doubling.)*

5.79   Continue as in the preceding frame.

5.80   Continue as in the preceding frame.

The descending form of the melodic minor scale *(or natural minor)*.

5.81   Refer, again, to the example in the preceding frame. What type of minor scale is used in the soprano voice?

_____

_____

5.82   The melodic minor scale provides alternate sixth and seventh scale degrees.

THE C MELODIC MINOR SCALE

The two forms of the melodic minor scale are used to provide tonal variety, and to avoid the melodic interval of an augmented second which is characteristic of the harmonic minor scale.

(No response.)

5.83   Note the use of the ascending form of the melodic minor scale below:

Beethoven, *Symphony No.* 7, Op. 92

Allegretto

The raised sixth degree of the melodic minor scale is used primarily to avoid the melodic interval of the augmented second which

harmonic

occurs in the _____ minor scale.

5.84   Write the alto and tenor voices. Supply, also, the Roman numeral analysis. *(Be sure the quality of each triad is reflected by the type of Roman numeral used.)*

d: i   IV   vii°6   i

d:

5.85   Continue as in the preceding frame.

g: i   III+   VI ii°6   V

g:

5.86   Continue as in the preceding frame.

f#:   i   v   i6 iv   V

f#:

5.87   Continue as in the preceding frame.

a: i   i6   IV vii°6 I

a:

5.88   When two or more triads in first inversion occur in succession, it often is impossible to use normal doubling in each chord. Notice the parallel fifths and octaves in the example below:

Successive first inversions often lead to the part writing error

of_____

incorrect parallel motion.
(Or equivlent.)

5.89   Normal doubling sometimes can be achieved by doubling the soprano in various voices.

The choice of doubling in such a case is determined by expediency. Alternate doublings are acceptable if they contribute to smooth part writing, or are necessary to avoid incorrect parallel motion. Judged by the above statements, which is the least objectionable,

parallel octaves or irregular doubling?_____

Irregular doubling.

5.90   Notice in the example below that various pairs of voices are doubled.

Bach, Chorale: *O Herre Gott, dein göttlich Wort*

List the triad tone (root, third, fifth) which is doubled in each chord.

Doubled tone

(1)   Third

(1) _____

(2)   Root

(2) _____

(3)   Fifth

(3) _____

E

(E is the leading tone in the key of F major.)

5.91   For the sake of effective melodic lines in each voice and to avoid incorrect use of parallel motion, irregular doubling often occurs when several chords in first inversion are used in succession. Active tones, however, should not be doubled. An active tone is one which has a strong tendency to resolve in one specific direction. The leading tone, for example, tends to resolve up a half-step to the tonic. Notes which are inflected chromatically are active in the direction of the inflection.

In the key of F major, which tone is more active, A or E?_____

5.92   Write the alto and tenor voices. Supply, also, the Roman numeral analysis.

e: i   i⁶   vii°⁶   i

e: ___   ___   ___   ___

                    6   ♭6

5.93   Write the alto and tenor voices. Supply, also, the Roman numeral analysis.

D: I   iii⁶   ii⁶   I⁶   V

D: ___   ___   ___   ___   ___

              6   6   6

(see next page)

or

D: I   iii⁶   ii⁶   I⁶   V

There are several possible solutions to this exercise, For this reason two answers are given. If your solution does not agree with either of these, check carefully for parallel fifths or octaves and also for awkward leaps. If free from these errors, your answer may be as good as the ones given.

e: i   vii°⁶   i⁶   ii°⁶   V

Irregular doubling is necessary to avoid Aug 2nd.

5.94   Write the alto and tenor voices and supply the Roman numeral analysis.

e: ___ ___ ___ ___ ___

5.95   Write the alto and tenor voices and supply the Roman numeral analysis.

C: I   I⁶   IV⁶   V⁶   I

C: ___ ___ ___ ___ ___

5.96   What part writing errors can you find in the following example? _____

_____

_____

_____

There are parallel fifths between the alto and tenor, and parallel octaves between the tenor and soprano in the second and third chords. There are also parallel octaves between the soprano and bass in the last two chords.

■   5.97   What part writing error is contained in the example below?

The leading tone (C♯) is doubled in the next-to-the-last chord (or the third of the diminished triad is *not* doubled).

_____

_____

5.98   The leading tone is highly active; it is attracted strongly to the tonic, which is merely a half-step higher. By doubling the leading tone, two voices are motivated in the same direction. Parallel motion results if both voices move to the tonic; if not, the activity of the leading tone is denied in one voice. In either case, undesirable voice leading results. This explains the rule: "*do not double the leading tone.*"

Two other points to bear in mind are these:

1.   Parallel fifths, unisons and octaves are forbidden.
2.   Avoid unnecessary leaps. *(Rarely is it necessary for a voice to leap more than a fourth.)*

(No response.)

5.99   The SECOND INVERSION of triads* is not used as frequently as either root position of first inversion. Triads in second inversion are used chiefly as part of a few specific harmonic progressions or musical textures. Since their use is relatively limited, it is fairly simple to establish the principles which govern their use.   Learn this:

PRINCIPLE 5

When a triad is in second inversion, double the bass.

(1)   (2)   (3)   (4)

Which triad tone is doubled in each case above? The (root/3rd

5th

/5th) _____.

_____

*Triads in second inversion are often referred to as six-four chords after the figured bass symbol $\frac{6}{4}$ which represents them.

---

(1)   (2)   (3)

5.100   Write the alto and tenor voices. Use *close structure* for each chord.

(1)   (2)   (3)

---

(1)   (2)   (3)

5.101   Write the alto and tenor voices. Use *close structure* for each chord.

(1)   (2)   (3)

5.102   Write the alto and tenor voices. Use *open structure* for each chord.

5.103   Write the alto and tenor voices. Use *open structure* for each chord.

5.104   Most second inversions fall into four patterns. From these patterns second inversion triads derive their names: CADENTIAL SIX-FOUR, PASSING SIX-FOUR, PEDAL SIX-FOUR, AND ARPEGGIO SIX-FOUR.

As the name implies, the CADENTIAL SIX-FOUR chord most often occurs at or near a cadence. (See NOTE.)

The example which begins below and continues on the following page includes a cadential six-four chord. Supply the Roman numeral analysis for the last two chords.

Mozart, *Sonata*, K. 331

$$\text{vi}^7 \qquad \text{V}^6 \qquad\qquad \text{I} \qquad \text{ii}^6 \text{\_\_\_ \_\_\_}$$

Note: A cadence is the close of a harmonic or melodic phrase. Cadences are presented in Chapter 6.0

$\text{I}^6_4 \qquad \text{V}$

5.105   Most second inversion triads perform a nonessential function due to their relatively unstable sonority.

Play at the piano (or from the recording) the example in the preceding frame. Focus your attention upon the effect of the last two chords.

Notice that the tonic six-four chord sounds almost incidental; it could be eliminated altogether by resolving into the dominant on the fourth eighth-note of the measure without changing drastically the harmonic effect. Many six-four chords are the result of nonharonic tones* or are used merely to delay resolution into a stronger chord.

The tonic six-four chord in the preceding frame delays momentar-

dominant

ily resolution into the _____chord.

*Nonharmonic tones are tones which are not part of the harmony. The various types of nonharmonic tones are presented in Chapter 9.0

5.106   The CADENTIAL SIX-FOUR chord occurs on a strong beat or a strong portion of a beat. The tonic six-four which resolves in the dominant (demonstrated in Frame 5.104) is the most common type. A second type of cadential six-four is shown below:

Bach, Chorale: *Gott sei uns gnädig und barmherzig*

$$\begin{array}{cc} \begin{smallmatrix}6\\4\end{smallmatrix} & \begin{smallmatrix}5\\\#\end{smallmatrix} \\ \text{f\#: iv}^6_4 & \text{I} \end{array}$$

tonic

In this case the subdominant six-four chord causes the ultimate resolution to the tonic chord to be delayed. With respect to harmonic function, the cadential six-four chord is "unessential." It is used to sustain activity by delaying resolution to either the dominant or the _____ chord.

False.
(Cadential six-four chords occur only on strong beats.)

5.107   Cadential six-four chords may occur on any beat regardless of the meter. (True.False) _____

5.108   The examples of cadential six-four chord which are shown in Frames 5.104 and 5.106 demonstrate the voice leading which is normally used.

Two of the upper voices move DOWN BY STEP.

THE CADENTIAL SIX-FOUR

$$\text{C:} \quad \text{I}^6_4 \qquad \text{V} \qquad\qquad \text{I}$$

In the example above, the usual resolution of the cadential six-four chord is reflected by the figured bass symbol: the sixth above the bass moves to the fifth, and the fourth above the bass moves to

third

the _____.

5.109   Write the alto and tenor voices. Supply the Roman numeral analysis.

g:

g: ___ ___ ___ ___ ___ ___

5.110   Write the alto and tenor voices. Supply the Roman numeral analysis.

D: I   ii⁶   I⁶₄   V   I

D: ___ ___ ___ ___ ___

5.111   Write the alto and tenor voices. Supply the Roman numeral analysis.

A♭:   I   ii⁶   I⁶₄   V

A♭: ___ ___ ___ ___

5.112   Write the alto and tenor voices. Supply the Roman numeral analysis. *(Write all chords in close structure.)*

B♭:   I   IV⁶   V   IV⁶₄   I

B♭: ___ ___ ___ ___ ___

5.113   *Summary of principles governing the use of cadential six-four chords*:

1.   The cadential six-four chord occurs in a pattern of two chords over the same bass note. There are two patterns:

     (a)   over the dominant (I_4^6 - V)

     (b)   over the tonic (IV_4^6 - I)

2.   The cadential six-four occurs on a *strong beat* of the measure or on a *strong portion of a beat*. The resolution occupies a relatively weak position.

3.   The upper voices which move upon the resolution of a cadential six-four usually move *down by step*.

     In a typical cadential six-four pattern, is the six-four chord as

No.

stable a sonority as the chord which follows it? _____

5.114   In terms of principles stated in the preceding frame, the cadential six-four chord in the example below is used incorrectly for two reasons. What are these errors?

(1)   The upper voices resolve upward rather than downward;

(1) _____

_____

(2)   The six-four chord should occur on a strong beat.

(In your own words.)

(2) _____

_____

5.115   Irregularities in the resolution of cadential six-four chords sometimes are caused by melodic considerations.

Mozart, *Quartet*, K. 387

Molto allegro

No.	In the preceding example, do any of the upper voices resolve "normally" (down by step)? _____
down	5.116 The "irregularities" in the resolution of the cadential six-four shown in the preceding frame are justified by the more emphatic effect which results. You see demonstrated here (as often is the case) that melodic requirements take precedence over such considerations as doubling, spacing, and normal resolution. Principles have been established to guide you in such matters, but they are not absolute rules, and practical necessity of the desire to produce more effective melodic lines occasionally will cause you to ignor them. In the "normal" resolution of the cadential six-four chord, the upper voices which move usually move (up/down) _____by step.
root	5.117 Below is an example of a PASSING SIX-FOUR chord. Brahms, *Ein deutsches Requiem*, Op. 45, IV Mäszig bewegt In this example the passing six-four chord is used to connect a triad in first inversion with the same triad in _____position.

5.118   Most passing six-four chords occur on a weak beat and connect either a triad in first inversion with the same triad in root position (as in the preceding frame), or the reverse. Both of these patterns are shown below:

(1)

(2)

G: I⁶   V⁶₄   I

g: iv   i⁶₄   iv⁶

No.

Does irregular doubling occur in any of the chords? _____

5.119   The passing six-four may appear between the root position and first inversion of any chord, but it is most often associated with either the tonic or subdominant chords.
   Write the alto and tenor voices and supply the Roman numeral analysis.

d: iv   i   V⁶₄   i⁶   V

d: __   __   __   __   __

5.120   Write the alto and tenor voices and supply the Roman numeral analysis.

D: I   IV⁶   I⁶₄   IV   vii°⁶   I

D: __   __   __   __   __   __

Bb: I   IV I$^6_4$ IV^6 V^6 V   vi

5.121   Write the alto and tenor voices and supply the Roman numeral analysis.

$^6_4$ 6   6

Bb: ___ ___ ___ ___ ___ ___ ___

---

e: i   V$^6_4$ i^6 ii$^{°6}$ V   i

5.122   Write the alto and tenor voices and supply the Roman numeral analysis.

(Note that the chord at the asterisk is a diminished triad. Double appropriately.)

$^6_4$ 6   6

e: ___ ___ ___ ___ ___ ___

(No response.)

5.123   Most passing six-four chords occur in the chord patterns below *(the reverse order is equally good):*

C: I   V$^6_4$ I^6

C: IV   I$^6_4$ IV^6

Notice that, except for inversion, the first and last chords are the same.

5.124   The PEDAL SIX-FOUR chord* is demonstrated twice in the example below. Supply the Roman numeral analysis of the first five chords.

Schumann, *Album for the Young*, Op. 68, No. 11

a: ___   ___ ___   ___ ___   V⁷   i

*The pedal six-four chord is related to a nonharmonic tone device called *pedal* or *pedal point*. This is presented in Chapter 9.0 (Frame 9.105–.110). Other terms for the pedal six-four chord used by some writers are *embellishing* six-four, *auxilliary* six-four and *stationary* six-four.

(Allegretto)

a: i   iv⁶₄ i   iv⁶₄ i   V⁷ i

subdominant

5.125   Another example of the pedal six-four chord is shown at the asterisk below:

Mozart, *Sonata*, K. 545

Allegro

C: I   V⁴₃   I

IV⁶₄   I   V⁶ V⁴₃   I

The pedal six-four chord occurs over the same (or repeated) bass note. It rarely is used except over the tonic, so the chords

usually involved are the tonic-_____-tonic.

a: i   iv$_4^6$ i   ii°^{6} i$_4^6$ V   VI

1. *a diminished triad*
2. *3rd is doubled to avoid*
parallel 5ths and 8ves.

5.126   Write the alto and tenor voices and supply the Roman numerals.

$_4^6$ $_3^5$ 6   6   ♯

a: ___ ___ ___ ___ ___ ___ ___

G: I   IV$_4^6$ I   IV^6 I^6 V

5.127   Write the alto and tenor voices and supply the Roman numeral analysis.

$_4^6$ $_3^5$ 6   6

G: ___ ___ ___ ___ ___ ___

5.128   If the tones of a chord are sounded successively rather than simultaneously, the result is an *arpeggio*. The ARPEGGIO SIX-FOUR is produced by arpeggiation in the bass. The chord at the asterisk is an arpeggio six-four.

Beethoven, *Quartet*, Op. 18, No. 2

Adagio cantabile

6   6
    4

(No response.)

The arpeggio six-four usually falls on a weak beat or weak portion of a beat and is preceded by the same chord in either root position or first inversion.

5.129   Arpeggiation is a prominent feature in piano music of the nineteenth century. It results in rich sonorous effects due to the large number of strings which can be caused to vibrate and rhythmic animation. The arpeggio six-four, particularly in piano music, is often merely illusion. When the damper pedal is depressed, all the strings are permitted to vibrate; thus the lowest tone continues to supply the foundation for the chord. Such a case is illustrated below:

Chopin, *Prelude*, Op. 28, No. 6

piano

The arpeggio six-four occurs frequently in music for the _____.

5.130   Write the alto and tenor voices and supply the Roman numeral analysis.

5.131   Write the alto and tenor voices and supply the Roman numeral analysis.

(Use the same quarter-note rhythm as in the soprano voice.)

5.132   Write the alto and tenor voices and supply the Roman numeral analysis.

(Use regular doubling for each chord.)

5.133   Write the alto and tenor voices and supply the Roman numeral analysis.

Summary

When all or most of the chords are in root position, the bass line tends to be angular. Inversions help smooth out the bass and thus enhance its melodic character. Inversions also provide variety with respect to chordal sonority. The interplay of sonorities that results from chords in various positions and inversions contributes significantly to the musical effect.

Care should be taken not to use chords in second inversion too frequently. Because they have relatively weak sonority, their use is limited mainly to the four standard types presented in this chapter (cadential, passing, pedal and arpeggio). Six-four chords were used more frequently and with greater freedom as the nineteenth century progressed; they nevertheless constitute only a small percentage of the total. First inversions, however, occur frequently. Their slightly unstable effect gives a sense of forward motion to the harmony. This is especially true when the chord is approached from a chord with a different bass note.

These additional principles should generally be followed for the doubling of triads in first and second inversion:

PRINCIPLE 4:   When a major or minor triad is in first inversion, the *soprano* is usually doubled.

EXCEPTION 4:   When a diminished triad is in first inversion, the *bass* is doubled.

PRINCIPLE 5:   When a triad is in second inversion, the bass is doubled.

Note: *Principle 5 does not have an exception.*

THE FOUR TYPES OF SIX-FOUR CHORDS.

Mastery Frames

5–1.   Identify the triad position indicated by each of the following figured bass symbols.

(1)   First inversion

(1)   6 _____

(2)   Second inversion

(2)   6
      4 _____

(3)   Root position

(3)   5
      3 _____

(5.1–.28)

5–2.   Complete the triads as indicated by the figured bass symbols.

(5.15–.20)

5–3   Complete the triads as indicated by the figured bass symbols.

(5.21–.25)

5–4   Write the appropriate Roman numeral for each triad. *Indicate inversions.*

(1)   a: vii°⁶

(2)   B♭:   I⁶₄

(3)   c: iv⁶

                              (5.33–.37)

a: ___   B♭: ___   c: ___

5–5   Write the appropriate Roman numeral for each triad. *Indicate inversions.*

(1)   D: IV⁶₄

(2)   F♯:   V⁶

(3)   d: III⁺⁶₄

                              (5.33–.37)

D: ___   f♯: ___   d: ___

5–6   Write the alto and tenor voices. *Use open structure.*

6   6   5
           4   ♯
                    (5.38–.116)

6   6   5
           4   ♯

5–5   The example in the preceding frame contains a cadential six-four chord. Name the three additional types of six-four chords.

(1)   Passing

(2)   Pedal

(3)   Arpeggio
(Any order.)   (5.106–.133)

(1)   _____

(2)   _____

(3)   _____

Supplementary Assignments

ASSIGNMENT   5–1   Name_____

1.   Indicate the note that will be in the lowest voice for each of the various positions of the designated triads.

TRIADS	B♭ MAJOR	C♯ MINOR	A♭ MAJOR
Root Position			
First Inversion			
Second Inversion			

2.   Place each triad in the proper category by listing numbers.

Root position: _____

First inversion: _____

Second inversion: _____

Bach, chorale: *Wer weiss, wie nahe mir* (altered)

3. When a major or minor triad is in first inversion the doubled voice normally is the _____.

4. Diminished triads are usually in first inversion with the _____ voice doubled.

5. When triads are in second inversion the doubled voice normally is the _____.

6. Write the chords indicated by the figured bass symbols. *(Use correct doubling and spacing.)*

(A)

(B)

7. Supply the proper chord symbols.

F: ___ ___ ___ ___   e: ___ ___ ___ ___ ___

8. Write the alto and tenor voices and provide the Roman numeral analysis.

Eb: ___ ___ ___ ___ ___ ___ ___

ASSIGNMENT 5–2   Name_____

1. Name the type of second inversion illustrated in each example.

    (1) _____   (3) _____

    (2) _____   (4) _____

2. Which is the least preferred version? _____

3. Which is the preferred version? _____

4. Write the alto and tenor voices and provide the Roman numeral analysis.

(A)

D:

(B)

c:

(C)

a:

5. Respond appropriately.

A. What is the quality of the first chord?

_____

B. Name the 6-4 chord type. _____

C. Why is the 6-4 chord incorrectly written?

_____

b:

D. Does the V chord resolve as expected? _____

Chapter 6.0
Phrase Structure and Cadences

The organized sounds of music elicit a variety of responses — sensual, emotional and intellectual; thus, music may be viewed as a form of communication. Like all communication intended for human consumption, music must take into account the listener's limited attention span. This causes musical ideas to be presented in digestible portions and punctuated in a manner comparable to the chapters, paragraphs, sentences and phrases of literature. The basic formal unit in music is the *phrase,* and phrases are set off from one another by *cadences.* Cadences provide moments of repose, as well as points of orientation.

Another elemental facet of communication in music is the use of *tension* and *relaxation* to arouse varying types and degrees of emotional response. Tension derives from: harmony, rhythm, timber, dynamics, texture and melodic contour. In this chapter we shall focus on the contribution of melodic contour to phrase structure. The role of harmonic cadences as terminators of phrases will also be stressed.

6.1   Music is organized into segments of various lengths and the basic unit of organization is the PHRASE. Most phrases in traditional music are four measures long. The four-measure phrase is so prevalent (especially during the classical period), that it can be regarded as the "normal" phrase length. Nevetheless, phrases both longer and shorter occur.

One of the basic units of formal organization is the

phrase

_____.

6.2   Another reason for the organization of music into relatively small units is the fact that, until the rise of pure instrumental music during the seventeenth and eighteenth centuries, music had a predominantly vocal orientation. Even in instrumental music the influence of vocal style continued to be felt until the end of the nineteenth century. Obviously, music which is intended for voices must provide breathing places for the performers. Since instrumental style has long been a reflection of vocal writing, it tends to have the same sort of organization. Breathing places are necessary for the comfort of the listener, too, as there is a tendancy to breath empathetically with the performer.

The phrase is a basic unit in the formal organization of music.* While phrases vary in length, their duration is usually about as long as a vocalist comfortably can sustain his or her breath. This is due to

vocal

the predominantly _____ orientation of music during the period of tonal harmony.

---

*Rudimentary information regarding phrase structure is presented here as it is vital to the understanding of certain aspects of harmony.

6.3   Shaping elements of the phrase include rhythm, harmony and melodic contour. The ascending and descending intervals of a melody produce lines, most of which fall into a few simple types. These types will be introduced in the next few frames.

The melody below ascends from a relatively low pitch to a higher level.

Tchaikovsky, *Symphony No. 4*, Op. 36

Andantino (più mosso)

Contour: _____

The "shape" of a melody — the line which is traced by its

various pitches — is called melodic _____.

contour

6.4   Another simple melodic contour is shown below:

Franck, *Symphonic Variations*   (1885)

Poco Allegro (più lento)

Contour: _____

This contour is the reverse of that shown in the preceding frame. Sing or play these two melodies. Which do you feel gives the more pronounced feeling of repose? (Frame 6.3/Frame 6.4)

_____

You are entitled to your own opinion, but see next frame.

6.5   Under most circumstances an ascending melodic line generates tension whereas a descending line provides relaxation. Ebb and flow of tension is an important element of musical expression, and one way tensions and relaxations are produced is through the contour of melodic lines.

ascending

descending

Normally tension is produced by an _____ line, relaxation by a _____ line.

6.6   The melody below illustrates a contour which occurs very frequently. This contour embodies the principle of tension followed by relaxation; the result is a sense of completion — a satisfying musical experience in miniature.

Mendelssohn, *Songs Without Words*, Op. 62, No. 4

Contour:

Contour:

(*No response.*)

6.7   Draw a profile beneath the melody below which illustrates its contour.

Brahms, *Symphony No. 4*, Op. 98

Contour:

(3).

6.8 The contour illustrated in the preceding frame is the reverse of that in Frame 6.6 and is not as common.
The four basic contours presented thus far are:

(1) _____   (3) ⌒

(2) _____   (4) ⌣

Which of these contours best expresses tension followed by

relaxation? _____

■

6.9 The combination of (3) and (4) of the preceding frame produces a fifth contour.

In this case, the melody extends both upward and downward from a central axis. Observe the melody below:

Haydn, *String Quartet*, Op. 3, No. 5

Scherzando

p

The note C is the axis and both the upper and lower limit is the

F

note _____.

■

6.10 Often rhythmic activity comes momentarily to a halt at the end of a phrase. Longer note values (and sometimes rests) are used at phrase endings to provide the desired degree of repose.
The example consists of two phrases; the asterisks denote the end of each.

Dvořák, *Symphony No. 9, Op. 95*

The desired degree of repose at the ends of phrases results from

rhythmic

the contour of the line, but also from a lessening of the _____ activity.

6.11   We shall continue by focusing upon how phrases end. As points of repose, cadences are extremely important to the study of harmony. Because they are goals of the phrase itself, cadences have special structural significance. The ear tends to listen for these goals, and relate surrounding material to them. The ends of phrases are called CADENCES.*   Learn this:
Cadences are melodic-harmonic formulas which bring phrases to a more or less definite close.
The points of repose which occur at the ends of phrases are called

cadences

_____.

*The word cadence comes from the Latin root word *cadere*, to fall. The term is descriptive of the most prevalent melodic contour at the ends of phrases (especially in monophonic music such as Gregorian chant).

6.12   There are two types of cadences: final and non-final.* Final cadences bring a phrase to a complete close. Non-final cadences point forward; they do not conclude a musical idea, but require yet another phrase to resolve their non-final effect.
List the two basic types of cadences.

(1)   Final

(1) _____

(2)   Non-final

(2) _____

*Final and non-final might also be described as terminal and progressive cadences respectively.

6.13   There are two final cadences and two non-final cadences.

FINAL CADENCES   NON-FINAL CADENCES

Authentic   Half
Plagal   Deceptive

Authentic and plagal cadences impart a sufficient degree of finality to close an entire composition, or an important section. Half and deceptive cadences, on the other hand, lack finality; they can be compared with the colon (:) or the question mark (?), both of which are punctuation marks which imply further elaboration.

Name the two cadences which may close an entire composition.

(1)   Authenic

(1)   _____

(2)   Plagal
(Any order.)

(2)   _____

6.14   The chords which produce each of the four cadences are shown below:

Authentic: V or vii° - I

Plagal: IV - I

Half: I, IV, or ii - V

Deceptive: V - vi

It is surprising that such a limited repertoire of cadences has sufficed for the huge mass of music which is based on tonal harmonic principles. Yet these four cadences have remained valid and have proved their usefulness in the music of several centuries.

Perhaps the continued popularity of tonal music is due, in part, to the orientation provided the listener by only a few cadence types, whose function (final or non-final) is so easily perceived. By virtue of their common use over a long period of time, these cadences provide the listener with points of reference regarding the function of a particular phrase in relation to the musical structure as a whole.

(No response.)

6.15   The AUTHENTIC CADENCE occurs more frqequently than any other. It is the strongest and most conclusive cadence. The authentic cadence consists of the chords V-I (V-i in a minor key).

Haydn, *The Creation*, No. 3

The cadence consists of the final two chords (V-I); but, as is shown in the example above, the tonic in second inversion (the cadential six-four) often is included as part of the cadential formula.
What are two chords which produce the authentic cadence?

_____ - _____ .

V-I
(orV-i).

6.16   Another authentic cadence is shown below:

Beethoven, *Symphony No. 8*, Op. 93

Allegro

F: V   V   I

Compare the cadence above with the ones shown in the preceding frame. Both are authentic cadences, but they do not have the same degree of finality.
Which do you think produces the stronger sense of conclusion?

(Frame 6.15/ 6.16) _____ .

Frame 6.15
(*There should be not doubt, but consider why.*)

6.17   Rhythm contributes to making the cadence of Frame 6.15 sound more conclusive than the cadence of Frame 6.16, but another factor is that the root of the tonic triad is in the soprano in the first case whereas the third is in the soprano in the second.
   The cadence in Frame 6.15 is a PERFECT authentic cadence whereas the cadence in Frame 6.16 is an IMPERFECT authentic cadence. The terms *perfect* and *inperfect* refer to the degree of finality

imparted by a _____ .

cadence

6.18   To qualify as a PERFECT cadence, the following conditions must be met:

(1)   Both chords must be in root position.

(2)   The final tonic chord must have the root in the soprano.

Why is the example on the next page *not* a perfect authentic

cadence? _____

_____

The dominant chord is not in root position.

The final chord has the third in the soprano.

6.19   Why is the cadence below *not* a perfect authentic cadence?

_____

_____

(2).

6.20   Which of the cadences below is a perfect authentic

cadence? _____

(3).

■ 6.21 Which of the following is a perfect authentic cadence?

_____

(1)   (2)   (3)

g: ii°⁶ V   i⁶   D: ii   V⁶   I   c: i   V   i

(2).

■ 6.22 Which of the cadences below is a perfect authentic

cadence? _____

(1)   (2)   (3)

G: I⁶ V   I   B♭: IV⁶ V   I   f: iv   V   i

■ 6.23 The final tonic triad of an authentic cadence in a minor key sometimes is altered to become a major triad. The raised third which produces this effect is called a PICARDY THIRD.

Bach, Chorale: *Das neugeborne Kindelein*

g: i⁶₄   V   I

The Picardy third causes a minor tonic to become a

major   _____ triad.

6.24 The PICARDY THIRD usually is reserved for the final cadence of a composition or an important section. It generally is felt that a major triad concludes a composition more strongly than a minor triad.

Play the example in the preceding frame substituting B-flat for B-natural in the final chord. Compare the effect of this version with the original. Which do you think is the stronger? (B-flat, or

B-natural) _____

You are entitled to your opinion . Certainly the B-natural produced the "brighter" sound.

6.25 Write the alto and tenor voices in accordance with the figured bass symbols. Analyze with Roman numerals.

d: i   iv   V   I

d: __ __ __   __

6.26 The cadence in the preceding frame is a perfect authentic

cadence with a PICARDY THIRD. (True/False) _____

True.

6.27 Write the alto and tenor voices in accordance with the figured bass symbols. Analyze with Roman numerals.

f#:   i   iv$^6_4$ i   V^6 I

f#:   __ __ __   __

6.28 The cadence in the preceding frame is a perfect authentic

cadence with a PICARDY THIRD. (True/False) _____

False.
(There is a Picardy third, but the cadence is imperfect.)

6.29   Check (√) the correct option:
1.   The PICARDY THIRD generally occurs in the authentic cadence in a minor key.
2.   The PICARDY THIRD occurs only in the perfect authentic cadence.

True statements:

(1) √

(1) _____   (2) _____   Both _____   Neither _____

■   6.30   The cadence vii°-I is also an authentic cadence.

Sibelius, *Finlandia*, Op. 26

Allegro moderato

Ab: vii°6   -   I

The vii°-I cadence is classed as an *imperfect* cadence; it does not convey as strong a sense of finality as the perfect authentic cadence (V-I).

The terms perfect and imperfect refer to the degree of finality of a cadence. Since the vii°-I cadence is "weaker" in effect than the V-I

imperfect

cadence, it is called an _____ authentic cadence.

■   6.31   The vii°-I cadence rarely is used for the final cadence of a composition, but it is useful for the close of phrases within a section. Another example of the vii°-I cadence is shown below:

Handel, Chorale: *Ach Gott und Herr,*
                        wie gross und schwer

C: ___   ___   ___   ___

C: I⁶ - IV - vii°6 - I

Analyze the example above with Roman numerals.

authentic

6.32   The leading tone triad (vii°) has virtually the same harmonic function as the dominant (V), so it may be substituted for V to

produce an imperfect _____ cadence.

6.33   The leading tone triad may be used to make an imperfect authentic cadence in a minor key.

Bach, Chorale: *Komm, Gott Schöpfer, heiliger Geist*

d: ___ ___ ___

d: IV - vii°6 - i
(Note the use of the ascending form of the melodic minor scale in this example.)

Supply the Roman numeral analysis for the last three chords.

6.34   Write the alto and tenor voices and analyze with Roman numerals.

g: i   V6   i vii°6 i

g: ___ ___ ___ ___ ___

6.35   Write the alto and tenor voices and analyze with Roman numerals.

f#:   i iv6 i IV vii°6 I

f#: ___ ___ ___ ___ ___

major (or) minor

6.36   Notice in the preceding frame that the ascending form of the melodic minor scale is used in the soprano voice. This is to avoid the augmented second (D to E-sharp) which would have occurred if harmonic minor had been used.

This example shows that in a minor key, depending upon whether or not the sixth scale degree is raised, the quality of the subdominant

triad may be either _____ or _____.

Picardy

6.37   Even though the example in Frame 6.35 is the key of F-sharp minor, the final chord contains an A-sharp. This device is called a

_____ third.

■

6.38   Write the alto and tenor voices and analyze with Roman numerals.

C: I   I⁶   IV   vii°⁶   I

C: ___   ___   ___   ___

■

6.39   Of the two "final" cadences (authentic and plagal). the authentic cadence is used much more frequently. The PLAGAL CADENCE has a "softer," less "positive" effect that the authentic cadence. The plagal cadence consists of the progression IV-I (iv-i in a minor key).

Brahms, *Symphony No. 1*, Op. 68

Più allegro

C: IV   I

(continued on next page)

The plagal cadence is a "final" cadence; it consists of the

IV - I   progression _____ - _____.

6.40   The plagal cadence is the familiar sound of the "Amen" which concludes most religious hymns.

Bourgeois, *"Old Hundredth"*

Praise   Fa - ther,   Son,   and

Ho - ly   Ghost.   A - men.

G: IV   I

The "Amen" cadence consists of the progression IV-I. Another

plagal   name for this cadence is the _____ cadence.

6.41   In a manner similar to the "Amen" cadence in the preceding frame, the plagal cadence often appears as an appendage after an authentic cadence. Used in this fashion, the plagal cadence "softens" the effect of the authentic cadence.

Chopin, *Etude*, Op. 25, No. 8

Db: V⁷ ___ ___ ___

I-IV-I

Supply the Roman numeral analysis for the final three chords.

6.42   Like authentic cadences, plagal cadences are perfect or imperfect depending upon the degree of finality. A perfect plagal cadence must end with the root of the final tonic chord in the soprano, and both chords (subdominant and tonic) must be in root position.
    Which of the cadences below is a *perfect plagal*

(3).

*cadence?*_____

Eb: IV⁶   I   IV   I   IV   I

(2).

6.43   Which of the cadences below is NOT a *perfect plagal*

cadence? _____

G: IV   I   d: iv   i   b: iv   i

a: i i⁶ vii°⁶ i iv i

6.44 Write the alto and tenor voices and analyze with Roman numerals.

Use close structure

                 6   ⌀

a: __ __ __ __ __ __

G: I vi I⁶ IV I

6.45 Write the alto and tenor voices and analyze with Roman numerals.

              6

G: __ __ __ __ __

c: i V⁶ i V iv i

6.46 Write the alto and tenor voices and analyze with Roman numerals.

        6   ♮

c: __ __ __ __ __

False *(It is an imperfect plagal cadence.)*	6.47 The cadence in the preceding frame is an imperfect authentic cadence. (True/False) _____
Both √	6.48 Check (√) the correct option: 1 Authentic and plagal cadences are final cadences. 2. A composition usually ends with a perfect cadence. True statements: (1) _____ (2) _____ Both _____ Neither _____
(2) √	6.49 Check (√) the correct option: 1. The progression vii°-I produces an imperfect plagal cadence. 2. Both authentic and plagal cadences may be either perfect or imperfect. True statements: (1) _____ (2) _____ Both _____ Neither _____
(No response.)	6.50 The two final cadences are *authentic* and *plagal*. These cadences are called *perfect* when the last two chords are in root position and the final tonic chord has the keynote in the highest voice. If these two conditions are not met, the effect of finality is weakened and the term *imperfect* is used. The terms *perfect* amd *imperfect* concern final cadences only. In the case of non-final cadences (half and deceptive), no terms are used to express the degree of finality.
	6.51 The HALF CADENCE is a non-final cadence; it concludes a phrase which is not a complete musical idea in itself and points forward toward yet another phrase. Schumann, *Album for the Young*, Op. 68. No. 4 Langsam

The final chord of a half cadence is usually the dominant.* It may be preceded by the tonic (as above) or any other chord which provides effective harmonic movement.

The progression ii-V produces a _____ cadence.

half

*Half cadences ending on the subdominant triad, while rare, do occur (See Frame 6.53.)

6.52   The cadential six-four often appears as part of a half cadence.

Beethoven, *Sonata*, Op. 49, No. 1

g: i   V$^6_5$ i   ___ ___ ___

Supply the Roman numeral analysis for the final three chords. *(Be sure the Roman numerals accurately reflect the quality of each triad.)*

ii°^{6} -i$^6_4$ - V

6.53   The half cadence which ends on the dominant triad is by far the most common type. Half cadences to the subdominant, although rare, provide an interesting effect.

Schumann, *Album for the Young*, Op. 68, No. 4

G: I   I^6 IV   ___ ___ ___ ___

Complete the Roman numeral analysis.

I - IV - vii°^{6} - I - IV

6.54 Check (√) the correct option;

1. The final chord of a half cadence may be IV or V, but V is much more common.

2. The chord preceding the final chord of a half cadence may be any chord which provides effective harmonic movement.

True statements:

(1) _____ (2) _____ Both _____ Neither _____

Both √

6.55 Write the alto and tenor voices and analyze with Roman numerals. *(Irregular doubling is necessary at the asterisk.)*

C: I   V^6 I   I^6 ii^6 V

(The 3rd was doubled at the asterisk to avoid parallel octaves between the soprano and tenor.)

C: ___ ___ ___ ___ ___

6.56 Continue as in the preceding frame. *(The chord at the asterisk should be in open structure. Write all other chords in close structure.)*

d: i   i i^6 iv   iv   V

d: ___ ___ ___ ___ ___

G: I   vii°⁶ I⁶ IV⁶   I⁶₄   V

6.57   Continue as in the preceding frame.

G: ___ ___ ___ ___ ___ ___

Bb: I   I   ii   vi   IV

6.58   Continue as in the preceding frame.

G: ___ ___ ___ ___ ___

Bb: ___ ___ ___ ___ ___

6.59   A special type of half cadence is shown below; it sometimes is called a PHRYGIAN CADENCE.*

Mendelssohn, Chorale: *Aus tiefer Noth schrei' ich zu dir*

f: iv⁶   V

---

*The term Phrygian is applied to the cadence above because it has the same basic structure as the true Phrygian cadence which occurs as vii-I in the Phrygian mode, i.e. the half-step (between D-flat and C) is similar to the half-step found between the first and second scale degrees of this mode. When used in the Phrygian mode, it is a final cadence. Traditional tonal harmony, however, is devoted so exclusively to major and minor tonalities that we shall continue to regard it as a type of half cadence.

half	The *Phrygian cadence* is most often a special type of _____ cadence.

■ 6.60   The Phrygian cadence consists of the progression iv-V in harmonic minor. There are two ways that it may be written.
These are shown below:

a: iv   V   iv⁶   V

The subdominant chord which precedes the final dominant in a Phrygian cadence may be in either root position or

_____ inversion.

first

■ 6.61   In the Phrygian cadence the root of the dominant chord is approached by step in contrary motion in the soprano and bass voices.

c: iv   V   c: iv⁶   V

Write the alto and tenor voices for (1) and (2) above.

6.62 Write the alto and tenor voices and analyze with Roman numerals.

e:

e: i   V⁶   i   iv⁶   V

6.63 The example in the preceding frame ends with a half cadence, but it is a special type of half cadence. It is a

Phrygian

_____ cadence.

6.64 The DECEPTIVE cadence is best understood by referring to the authentic cadence. When another chord is substituted for the final tonic, the expected resolution of the dominant is avoided.

(1) AUTHENTIC   (2) DECEPTIVE

G: __ __ __ __   G: __ __ __ __

(1) ii   I⁶   V   I

(2) ii   I⁶   V   vi

Analyze each of the above examples with Roman numerals.

6.65 In (2) of the preceding frame the submediant triad (vi) is substituted for the tonic. *This is by far the most common type of deceptive cadence.*
   The deceptive cadence is similar to an authentic cadence except that the dominant does not resolve to the tonic as expected. Although the final chord might be any one to which the dominant

submediant (vi)

could resolve, it usually is the _____.

6.66   Composers use the deceptive cadence for variety and to prolong harmonic interest. The deceptive cadence is not a final cadence; several additional chords (or a phrase or two) are required to give a sense of completion following a deceptive cadence.

Play the example below:

Bach, Chorale: *Es ist das Heil uns kommen her*

Bb: ii   I⁶   V   vi

Deceptive.

What type of cadence is shown above? _____

6.67   The deceptive cadence is very effective in a minor key.

Chopin, *Valse Brillante*, Op. 34, No. 2

Lento

a: V⁷   VI

In a major key the root of the submediant triad is a whole-step above the dominant, and the quality of the triad is minor. In a *minor* key the root of the submediant triad is a half-step above the domi-

major

nant, and the quality of the triad is _____.

6.68   You must take care when writing a deceptive cadence in a minor key that an augmented second does not appear in one of the voices.
Compare the following two examples:

In (1) an undesirable augmented second occurs in the alto. This is corrected in (2) by allowing the alto to double the soprano on the third of the submediant triad. This is the customary way to handle this problem.

In four-part writing the final submediant triad of a deceptive

third

cadence will almost always contain a doubled _____.

6.69 Write the alto and tenor voices and analyze with Roman numerals.
(Write all chords in close structure except for the final chord which must contain irregular doubling.)

6.70 Write the alto and tenor voices and analyze with Roman numerals.

F: I V I⁶ ii⁶ V vi

■ 6.71 Continue as in the preceding frame
(The chords at the asterisks should contain doubled thirds.)

F: __ __ __ __ __ __

D: I I⁶ IV I⁶₄ V vi

■ 6.72 Continue as in the preceding frame.

D: __ __ __ __ __ __

■ 6.73 To provide an extra element of surprise the submediant chord, which would normally appear in minor, sometimes is used in a major key.

Schubert, *Symphony No. 5 in B-flat Major*

Andante con moto

E♭: I⁶₄   V⁷   VI

The borrowing of a chord from a minor mode for use in its parallel major is discussed in Part II, Chapter 5.0: BORROWED

CHORDS. The example above is presented here as it illustrates a common type of deceptive cadence.

The element of surprise is an important feature of the

deceptive

_____ cadence.

_____

*The terms *modal exchange* or *change of mode* might be used by some writers, rather than *borrowed chord*, to describe this example.

6.74   *Write the alto and tenor voices.*
   (Watch for parallel fifths between the second and third chords. Remember, also, to double the final chord as if it were in the key of A minor.)

If you chose:

(a)   go to Frame 6.76

(b)   go to Frame 6.77

(c)   go to Frame 6.78

6.75   Which of the choices ((a), (b) or (c)) produces a correctly written *deceptive* cadence? _____

(No response.)

6.76   Choice (a) results in a chord which has incorrect doubling (there are two fifths). In addition, there are parallel fifths between the bass and tenor voices.

Return to Frame 6.75 and try again.

(No response.)

6.77   This choice (b) results in normal doubling for a minor triad in root position, but there is an augmented second in the soprano voice (F♯ -E♭). This interval should be avoided.

Return to Frame 6.75 and try again.

augmented second	6.78 You have made the correct choice. The third of the submediant triad must be doubled in the deceptive cadence in a minor key. This is to avoid the melodic use of an undesirable interval. What is this interval? The _____.
If you chose: (a) go to Frame 6.80 (b) go to Frame 6.81 (c) go to Frame 6.82	6.79 Which of the choices ((a), (b) or (c)) produces a correctly written *imperfect authentic* cadence? _____
(No response.)	6.80 Choice (a) results in an imperfect *plagal* cadence. *Return to Frame 6.79 and find the imperfect authentic cadence.*
The third of the final chord is in the soprano. *(Or equivalent.)*	6.81 You have made the correct choice. What makes this an *imperfect* cadence? _____ _____ *(Skip to Frame 6.82.)*
(No response.)	6.82 Choice (c) results in a *perfect* authentic cadence. *Review Frame 6.18 then return to Frame 6.79 and try again.*
(1) Half (2) Deceptive	6.83 The authentic and plagal cadences are "final" cadences. Name the two "non-final" cadences. (1) _____ (2) _____

Summary

One of the basic formal units of music is the phrase. The phrase is a segment of music that can be assimilated comfortably by the listener. The melodic aspect of a phrase is traced by the successive pitches. Raising pitches tend to create tension; falling pitches tend to relax tension.

Most melodic phrases are based on one of four contours; a fifth contour is a combination of the third and fourth. The basic contours are:

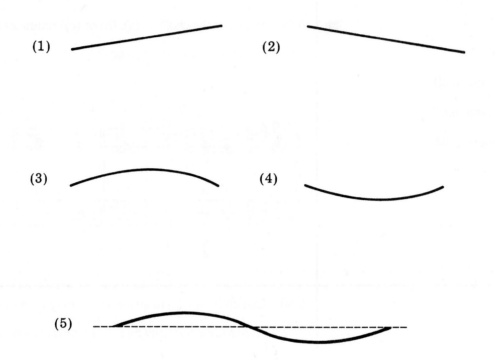

Cadences serve to punctuate the phrases which unite to build larger formal units. The four types of cadences (authentic, plagal, half, and deceptive) provide a very limited repertoire of punctuations. This is one reason why traditional music is easy for the listener to apprehend. Not only is the expressive significance of each cadence type clear, but tonal implications usually are unambiguous. Thus, frequent tonal orientations are provided the listener, and these orientations lend assurance that the path through tonal thickets is not lost.

It is useful to compare cadences with the punctuation marks used in writing.

PUNCTUATION		CADENCE
Period (.) Exclamation Point (!)	} =	Perfect Authenic and Perfect Plagal
Semicolon (;) Comma (,)	} =	Imperfect Authentic and Imperfect Plagal
Colon(:) Question Mark (?)	} =	Half and Deceptive

Of course you must regard this list as being merely suggestive. Musical expression is far too subtle to be neatly pinned down is this fashion, and the analogy between music and language should not be pressed too hard. On the other hand, you must acquire a sensitivity to the functions of the various types of cadences, and a personal reference of your own — similar to the one above — might be useful.

Mastery Frames

	6–1 Identify the type of cadence represented by the Roman numerals.
(1) Deceptive	(1) V - vi _____
(2) Plagal	(2) IV - I _____
(3) Authentic	(3) V or vii° - I _____
(4) Half (6.14)	(4) I, IV or ii-V _____

(2) Plagal (and)	6–2 List the cadences in the preceding frame that are final
(3) Authentic (6.13)	cadences. _____ and _____ .

	6–3 Name each of the cadences in the example below and analyze:
(1) Authentic	(1) _____
(2) Plagal	(2) _____
(1) e: iv V i	(1) e: __ __ __ (2) B♭: __ __
(2) B♭ : IV I	
(6.15–.50)	

(2). (6.17–.22)	6–4 Which example in the preceding frame shows an imperfect cadence? _____

6–5 Name each of the cadences below and analyze:

(1) Deceptive

(2) Half (or Phrygian)

    (1) _____

    (2) _____

(1) A: ii⁶ V vi

(2) d: i iv⁶ V

       6.51–.74)

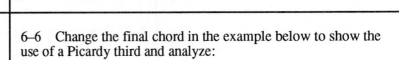

(1) A: __ __ __ (2) d: __ __ __

a: ii°₆ i⁶₄ V I

(6.23–.29)

6–6 Change the final chord in the example below to show the use of a Picardy third and analyze:

a: __ __ __ __

Supplementary Assignments

ASSIGNMENT 6–1   Name _____

1.   Compose single line melodies (four to eight measures long) that illustrate the specified melodic contours. Choose your own keys and meters. Indicate tempo, dynamics and phrasing. Each melody should be analyzed.

(1)   Ascending

(2)   Descending

(3)   Arch

(4)   Inverted arch

(5)   Axial

2.   Compose other melodies with your own specifications and analyze them.

3. Identify these cadences as final or non-final:

    Half   _____

    Authentic   _____

    Deceptive   _____

    Plagal   _____

4. Identify the cadences below and analyze:

Bb: __   __   A: __   __   G: __   __   f: __   __

5. The cadence produced by the chords iv-V (in minor) is called a _____cadence.

6. Identify the four cadences below and supply Roman numerals according to keys specified:

    (1) _____   (3) _____

    (2) _____   (4) _____

    B: __   __   d: __   __   Ab: __   __   f#: __   __

7. Compose and part write other examples of cadences with your own specifications and analyze them.

ASSIGNMENT 6–2   Name _____

1. Identify the cadences as either perfect or imperfect.

(1) _____   (2) _____

c#:   Eb:

Beethoven, *Symphony No. 8, Op. 93*

(3) _____   (4) _____

D: F:

2. Which example shows a Phrygian cadence? _____

(1)   (2)   (3)

d: C: e:

3. Compose two four-measure phrases based on the harmonic progression below. Write for the piano in homophonic texture. Refer to Appendix B, *Piano Styles*. (For this assignment, style 6 through 9 are recommended; use style 13 if you have more experience with piano.)

4. Compose two or more phrases of your own specification on your own staff paper. Write either for the piano or for instruments.

5. Answer the questions regarding the example below:

(Schumann)

(1) This example consists of only triads in either root position or second inversion. (True/False) _____

(2) The chords which are in second inversion are all of one type. Identify this type._____

(3) This example ends with a _____cadence.

(4) Which form of the minor scale is used in the example? _____

(5) Chord 7 is a tonic chord. Thus, it is an example of structural harmony. (True/False) _____

Chapter 7.0
Harmonic Progressions

The relation of chords to one another with in the structure of tonality was treated in Chapter 2.0. Our job now is to distinguish between progressive and retrogressive chord movement (movement of roots), and to examine various patterns of harmonic phrase structure (seccession of harmonies within a phrase). The work in this chapter will shed additional light on the shaping function of harmony, and prepare for the study of harmonization techniques which follows.

	7.1 The manner in which chords relate to one another lies at the heart of the study of tonal harmony. A series of chords is called a HARMONIC PROGRESSION. During the period of tonal harmony sufficient consistency is harmonic progression was shown that we may refer to a "language of harmony." A language is established by consistent use, and it is the consistencies in the harmonic language which shall be our chief concern. Even though the music of each composer in the period of tonal harmony speaks with a different "accent," the underlying principles are closely related. Harmonic progression is concerned with the way_____ relate to one another.
chords	
	7.2 The term *harmonic progression* refers in a general way to all harmonic movements. The term PROGRESSION, however, is applied to a particular type of harmonic action: one which gives a sense of "forward motion." Weaker harmonic relations which sometimes give a sense of "backward motion" are called RETROGRESSIONS. The terms PROGRESSION and RETROGRESSION distinguish between relatively "strong" and "weak" harmonic movements. A "strong" "emphatic" harmonic movement is called a _____.
progression	
	7.3 "Strong and "weak" are very subjective and inadequate words to describe the effect of various harmonic progressions. Above all, they should not be equated with "good" and "bad," for the expressive purpose of a particular passage may be served better by the use of retrogressions than by progressions. One of the ideals of harmony is variety, and too consistent a use of either progressions or retrogressions is undesirable. Harmonic variety is achieved by the use of both _____ and _____.
progressions (and) retrogressions	

7.4   You must now learn to distinguish between progressive and retrogressive harmonic movements.

The harmonic relationship of any two chords is classified according to the interval by which their roots are related.

Write in the space provided beneath each example the basic interval (2nd, 3rd, 4th, etc.) *between the roots* of the two chords.

(Determine first the root of each chord.)

(1)   5th (*or 4th*)

(2)   2nd

7.5   Continue as in the preceding frame.

(Determine first the root of each chord.)

(1)   3rd

(2)   5th (*or 4th*)

7.6   In the preceding two frames you were given the choice of analyzing some of the root movements as either down a fifth or up a fourth. Because of interval inversion, the root relationship in either case is the same.

The following example shows that the interval of a fourth up is the same as a fifth down, a sixth up is the same as a third down, and a seventh up is the same as a second down.

In order to simplify references to root movements, we shall speak of only three basic relationships: fifths, thirds and seconds.

third

Root movement up a sixth is the same as down a _____

second

7.7   Root movement up a seventh is the same as down a _____.

fourth

7.8   Root movement down a fifth is the same as up a _____.

up

7.9   Root movement down a seventh is the same as _____ a second.

7.10   Indicate the basic interval between the root of the chords in each case.
    (*Remember: The three relationships are fifths, thirds, and seconds.*)

(1)   2nd   (2)   5th

7.11   If your answer for (2) is the preceding frame was "4th," remember that a fourth up is the same as a fifth down. In this study, basic root relationships are to be analyzed as fifths,

thirds, (or) seconds

_____, or _____.

7.12 Indicate the basic interval between the roots of the chords in each case.

(1)   (2)

(1)   3rd   (2)   5th

—   —

7.13 Continue as in the preceding frame.

(1)   (2)

(1)   5th   (2) 2nd

—   —

■   **7.14** Do not confuse root movements with the melodic intervals shown in the bass voice.

Graun, Chorale: *Herzliebster Jesu, was hast du verbrochen*

(Roots)

The arrows show the direction of the interval, The symbol ↓ 5, for example, means that the root movement is down a fifth. Notice, too, that the root movement between the fourth and fifth chords is actually *up a sixth*. This is classified as *down a third*.

How would you classify root movement up a seventh? _____

Down a second.

_____

7.15   In order to classify root movements accurately you must locate the root of each chord. Do not be confused when some chords are in first or second inversion.

Write the roots and analyze with arrows and numbers (as in the preceding frame) each of the root movements in the example below.

(Remember: Up a fourth is classified as down a fifth.)

Bach, Chorale: *Von Gott will ich nicht lassen*

Rep. ↑5 ↓5 ↓5   ↓5 ↑3 ↓5

7.16   Continue as in the preceding frame. (*Note: When the root is repeated, abbreviate "Rep."*)

7.17   Chord movements are progressive or retrogressive depending upon the intervallic relation of their roots. N.B.: *Inversions do not affect progression/retrogression classification; it is ROOT relations which count.*

Analysis of music from the eighteenth and nineteenth centuries reveals a predominance of root movements *down in fifths, up in seconds* and *down in thirds*. The prevalence of these relationships has established a feeling of "progression" which contrasts with a feeling of "retrogression" when roots move otherwise.

List the root movements which result in PROGRESSIONS.

Down in fifths, up in seconds

(and) down in thirds.

_____,_____

and_____.

(3).

7.18   Which example below demonstrates a *progression*? _____

(*Take care not to be fooled by inversions.*)

(2).

7.19   Which example below demonstrates a *progression*? _____

7.20   The diagram below may help you to remember the progressions which occur when roots move *down in fifths:*

ROOT MOVEMENT DOWN IN FIFTHS

I
IV
vii°
iii
vi
ii
V
I

(*Note: In this diagram, as in others elsewhere in this book, the Roman numerals are given as for a major key. The progressions are equally valid in a minor key.*)

The mediant chord followed by the submediant is a progression

fifth

because the root movement is down a _____.

7.21   In the following example there are two progressions in which roots move *down in fifths*. Between which chords do these occur?

1 (and) 2

Between chords _____ and _____, and between

4 (and) 5

chords _____ and _____.

(*You may wish to locate the root of each chord on the empty staff provided for this purpose.*)

Brahms, *Symphony No. 1,* Op. 68

Andante sostenuto

7.22   The diagram below shows progression of roots moving *up in seconds*:

ROOT MOVEMENT UP IN SECONDS

I
vii°
vi
V
IV
iii
ii
I

Is the subdominant chord followed by the dominant a progression or a retrogression? A _____.

progression

7.23   In the following example, root move *up in seconds* twice. Between which chords do these progressions occur?

3 (and) 4

5 (and) 6

Between chords _____ and _____, and between chords _____ and _____.

(You may wish to locate the root of each chord on the empty staff provided for this purpose.)

Graun, Chorale: *O Traurigkeit, o Herzeleid*

7.24   The diagram below shows progressions of roots moving *down in thirds*.

ROOT MOVEMENT DOWN IN THIRDS

I
vi
IV
ii
vii°
V
iii
I

Roots moving down in thirds produce *progressions*. What term applies to root movements *UP in thirds*? _____

Retrogression.

7.25   When a chord moves to another chord whose root is a third higher, the new root is contained in the previous chord. This results in a weaker effect than when the root moves *down a third*. In this case the new root has not been heard previously; it is a new sound and the result is a "stronger" sense of progression.

(1) UP a 3rd   (2) DOWN a 3rd

subdominant (IV)	What chord follows the submediant (vi) if the root moves down a third? The _____.

7.26   Check (√) the correct option:

1. Harmonic movement from one chord to another is classified as either a progression or a retrogression depending upon the root movement.
2. It is desirable that all harmonic movement should be progressions.

True statements:

(1) _____   (2) _____   Both _____   Neither _____

(1) √

7.27   Check (√) the correct option:

1. Root movement up a sixth is the same as down a third.
2. Root movement up a fourth is the same as down a fifth.

True statement:

(1) _____   (2) _____   Both _____   Neither _____

Both √

7.28   All of the root movements listed below are progressions.

(True/False) _____

(1)   up a 2nd   (3)   down a 3rd
(2)   down a 2nd   (4)   up a 5th

False.
((2) and (4) are retrogressions.)

7.29   We have learned that *progressive* harmonic movement occurs when roots move down in fifths, up in seconds, or down in thirds. One other important principle remains to be stated:
   Harmonic movement from the tonic to any other chord is progressive regardless of the interval involved.
   In view of this statement, which case below shows progressive harmonic movement? _____

(2).

KEY OF D MAJOR

(1).
((2) is progressive because harmonic movement from the tonic to any other chord is progressive.)

7.30   Because the tonic triad is built on the key note it is the least active chord in any key. Thus, movement from the tonic to any other triad is movement to a *more active chord.*

Which example shows *retrogressive* harmonic

movement?_____

KEY OF G MINOR

(2)
(Root movement down a 2nd as in (1) is retrogressive.)

7.31   Which example shows *progressive* harmonic

movement?_____

KEY OF A MAJOR

True.

7.32   No retrogression is possible when moving from the tonic

chord. (True/ False) _____

True.

7.33   The sequence of chords represented by Roman numerals

below contains progressions only. (True/False) _____

I   IV   V   vi   IV   ii   V   I

7.34   Actually, no clear distinction between progression and retrogression can be made. Under most circumstances, harmony functions not as an isolated phenomenon, but in conjunction with rhythm and melody. The latter two elements may affect harmony so that a succession of chords sounds progressive in one case but retrogressive in another. Nevertheless, you must develop your sensitivity to various degrees of "progressiveness" in harmonic relations to acquire skill in selecting expressive harmonies.

Although the principles of harmonic progression are not absolutely clear, the tendency for roots to progress down in fifths, up in seconds, and down in thirds is prevalent enough in tonal music to serve as a guide in the choice of chords.

Few harmonic phrases consist entirely of either progressions or retrogressions. Fluctuation in the balance between these two types of harmonic movement provides the composer with an expressive tool. A passage in which stability and tonal clarity are desired calls for a large proportion of progressions, while more retrogressions might be used when the opposite effect is desired.

Harmony contributes to musical expression through the fluctuating balance between progressive and retrogressive harmonic movement.

(No response.)

7.35   We shall continue by exploring another approach to harmonic progression.

The structure of tonality rests upon the foundation of the three primary triads: the tonic, subdominant and dominant. The remaining triads are called secondary triads and are related to the primary triads in the manner shown below*

Primary triads: ⌈ I   ⌈ IV   ⌈ V
Secondary triads: ⌊ vi   ⌊ ii   ⌊ iii, vii°

Spell the primary triads in the key of E major.

I   -   EG♯B   I   -   _____

IV -   AC♯E   IV -   _____

V   -   BD♯F♯   V   -   _____

_____

*At this point you may wish to review Chapter 2.0: The Structure of Tonality.

7.36   Primary and secondary triads provide another approach to harmonic progressions.

Learn these two principles:

1. Movement from a primary triad to its secondary triad is *progressive.*

2. A secondary triad may be substituted for its primary triad.

    With respect to (1) above, which case below is a progression?

(3).

_____

(1)   I-iii   (2)   vi-I   (3)   IV-ii   (4)   iii-V

---

(2).

7.37   Which case below is a progression? _____

(1)   V-IV   (2)   I-vi   (3)   vii°-vi   (4)   vi-V

7.38   Applying the principle that primary triads tend to progress to their secondary triads rather than the reverse, show how each chord below would porgress.

(1)   vi

(2)   ii

(3)   iii (or) vii°

(1)   I   _____

(2)   IV   _____

(3)   V   _____ or _____

■

7.39   The harmonic relationships shown in the preceding frame are written out below:

(Play these progressions at the piano or listen to the recording.)

Bb: I   vi   IV   ii   V   iii   vii°6

Do you think these progressions are all equally effective?

Your opinion.

_____

7.40   Even when dealing with very simple musical material it is difficult to make absolute judgements; for not only are all elements relative and easily influenced by other factors, but honest and perfectly valid differences of opinion may be held by all of us.

Most of you will probably feel that all of the progressions shown in the preceding frame are effective with the possible exception of V-vii°. This is a relatively weak progression because the harmonic function of these two chords is so similar (vii° is considered by some to be an incomplete V^7) that little harmonic motion results when going from one to the other.*

Except for the progression V-vii°, movement from a primary triad to its secondary triad generally results in a strong harmonic

True.

effect. (True/False) _____

_____

*Note, too, that v-vii° is root movement up a third—-a retrogression.

7.41   A secondary triad may be substituted for its primary triad at any point in order to provide tonal variety and to prolong the harmonic motion.

Basic progression: $\begin{bmatrix} \text{I} \end{bmatrix} \begin{bmatrix} \text{V} \end{bmatrix} \begin{bmatrix} \text{I} \end{bmatrix}$

Substitutions: $\begin{bmatrix} \text{I} \end{bmatrix} \begin{bmatrix} \text{vii°} \end{bmatrix} \begin{bmatrix} \text{vi} \end{bmatrix}$

The basic progression (I-V-I) above is changed by substituting vii° for V, and vi for I. Further, the authentic cadence (V-I) has

deceptive

become a _____cadence (vii°-vi).

7.42   Applying the principle demonstrated in the preceding frame, show the chords which may be substituted where indicated below:

Basic progression: I ⌈ IV ⌈ I ⌈ V   I

Substitutions: I ⌊ __ ⌊ __ ⌊ __   I

ii-vi-vii° or iii*
_____
*Rarely used.

7.43   Continue as in the preceding frame.

Basic progression: I   V ⌈ I ⌈ IV   V ⌈ I

Substitutions: I   V ⌊ __ ⌊ __   V ⌊ __

vi-ii- (V)-vi

7.44   Continue as in the preceding frame.

Basic progression: I ⌈ V   I ⌈ I ⌈ IV   V ⌈ I

Substitutions: I ⌊ __   I ⌊ __ ⌊ __   V ⌊ __

vii° or iii*-(I)-vi-ii-(V)-vi
_____
*Rarely used.

(No response.)

7.45   The first principle stated in Frame 7.36 is that *movement from a primary triad to its secondary triad is progressive.* The second principle is that *a secondary triad may be substituted for its primary triad.*

The application of these principles results in a wide variety of chord progressions. This is shown below:

	(1)		(2)	
I	vi	IV	vii°	I

Movement from a primary triad to its secondary triad is shown at (1); at (2), the leading tone triad (vii°) is substituted for the dominant (V).

7.46   Indicate which of the two principles is used at each of the points indicated.

Principle 1.   Movement from a primary triad to its secondary triad.

Principle 2.   Substitution of a secondary triad for its primary triad.

	(1)		(2)		(3)		(4)	
I	ii	V	iii	IV	I	vi	IV	vii° I

(1)   Principle 2   (1)   _____

(2)   Principle 1   (2)   _____

(3)   Principle 1   (3)   _____

(4)   Principle 2   (4)   _____

7.47   Continue as in the preceding frame.

			(1)		(2)		(3)	
I	iii	IV	ii	V	vi	V	iii	I

(1)   Principle 1   (1)   _____

(2)   Principle 2   (2)   _____

(3)   Principle 1   (3)   _____

(No response.)

7.48   The primary triads (I, IV and V) serve as the structural basis for harmonic progressions, but basic formulas such as I-V-I and I-IV-V-I can be expanded by the use of secondary triads. This is done by moving from a primary triad to its secondary triad before proceeding to the next chord in the basic formula (I-V-I expanded to I-vi-V-I); or by substituting a secondary triad for its primary triad (I-IV-V becomes I-ii-V). The result is greater tonal variety through a wider choice of chords and in some cases, prolongation of the harmonic activity.

As we proceed with this study you must bear in mind that harmonic progression is not a science which can be presented in terms of precise laws. We shall make no attempt to relate harmony to natural acoustical phenomena even though much has been made of this approach in the past. This presentation is based upon the observed practices of composers who use the traditional harmonic vocabulary.

In this text principles are not stated as rules, but are intended to serve as guides for the development of your own personal command of harmonic materials.

Yes (certainly).

7.49   An intimate relation exists between harmonic progression and phrase structure. A phrase has *shape* through melodic contour and *motion* through rhythm. Also it has a beginning, a sense of growth or movement in a particular direction, and finally a point of arrival at the cadence.

Harmonic progressions, like melody, tend to focus upon the cadence. The cadence to which a harmonic phrase moves has a strong influence upon the choice of chords earlier in the phrase.

Cadences are structural points in a composition and the harmony at these points has special importance in the formal organization. Chords which appear at cadence points usually are chosen so that the tonal organization is stressed.

We have referred frequently to *melodic* phrases. Do you think it

would be appropriate to speak of *harmonic* phrases? _____

(No response.)

7.50   Some chords in a harmonic phrase are more important to the formal organization of music than others. These include the following:

1.   Chords which appear at structural points (cadences).

2.   Chords which are stressed rhythmically (on strong beats or strong portions of beats, prolonged, or emphasized by being preceded by a rest).

3.   Chords at important points in the phrase (at the peak of the melodic contour, for example).

Melodic contour, phrase structure and rhythm all have an influence upon the choice of chords.

7.51   Harmony which appears at strategic points and serves to establish the tonal organization is called STRUCTURAL HARMONY. Examine the excerpt below :

Beethoven, *Sonatina in G Major*

The analysis above shows the basic "structural" harmonic movement from the tonic to the dominant in measure four. This is followed by a phrase which begins and ends with tonic harmony.

Show with Roman numerals the *basic* harmonic organization of

this excerpt._____

I - V - I

7.52   Referring again to the example in the preceding frame, notice that the chords at structural points of lesser importance (Roman numerals in parentheses) also are primary triads (IV and V).

Harmony plays an important role in defining the tonal structure of music. As shown in the previous frame, this occurs at different levels even within the phrase itself. Harmony which is form-defining, and which helps to establish tonal coherence is called

_____ harmony.

structural

■ 7.53   Chords which occur more or less incidentally produce embellishing harmony. The first two measures of the excerpt in Frame 7.51 are shown below to illustrate this type of harmony.

Beethoven, *Sonatina in G Major*

Romanze

The dominant seventh chord on the second beat of the first measure is preceded and followed by tonic harmony. Thus, its function is clearly one of embellishment.

Is it likely that harmony at the end of a phrase would be

No.

embellishing? _____

7.54   *To achieve the delicate shades of nuance which fine performance demands, it is imperative that you recognize the difference between structural and embellishing harmony. The larger units in the formal organization of a composition are defined, in part, by structural harmony. The importance of structural harmony as opposed to embellishing harmony cannot be understated. By phrasing, performers must make clear the formal design of the music being played. To do this, a sensitivity to the various roles of harmony is vital.*

Harmony which is incidental and not form-defining is

embellishing

called_____ harmony.

■ 7.55   In this frame you have the delicate task of distinguishing between structural and embellishing harmony. Examine carefully the example below and play it at the piano. Each chord is numbered and analyzed with a Roman numeral. List in the space provided on the next page those chords which seem incidental to the basic harmonic scheme.

(Indicate your answer by recording the appropriate numbers.)

Beethoven, *Sonata*, Op. 49, No. 1

2, 6, 10, 13
(There may be some difference of opinion, but the following frame justifies this list.)

Embellishing harmony: Chords _____

7.56   A test which sometimes is useful to distinguish between structural and embellishing harmony is to play the passage omitting all embellishing harmony. Try the version below:

Beethoven, *Sonata*, Op. 49, No. 1 (altered)

Your answer is probably *No,* but you are entitled to you opinion.

Do you think the basic harmonic design of this passage has been affected by the elimination of chords 2, 6, 10, and 13? _____

■ 7.57   Some of you may feel that in the preceding frame too many chords were retained. A further reduction of the harmony follows:

Beethoven, *Sonata*, Op. 49, No. 1 (altered)

Now list (by number) all of the chords which have been deleted from the original version in Frame 7.55. *Embellishing harmony*:

2, 3, 4, 5, 6, 7, 10, 11, 12, 13

Chords _____

7.58   In the preceding frame so many chords are deleted from the original version that not all of the melodic notes are accommodated by those which remain. Yet the basic structure of the harmonic phrase is preserved. Further reduction in the number of chords would destroy the sense of harmonic movement.
    Structural harmony may be identified by eliminating

embellishing

all _____harmony.

7.59   The structure of music is built up, in part, by harmonic relationships. Harmony operates at many levels, and even the tonal relationships between the parts of multi-movement works are important. At the phrase level, harmony (along with cadences, melodic contour, rhythm and motivic development) serves to define form and give coherence to music.

The varying roles of harmony can be seen by stripping away the embellishing harmony layer by layer to reveal the different levels of the tonal structure. The harmony which remains is called *structural* harmony. A clear distinction between structural and embellishing harmony cannot always be made. This is a matter of personal opinion, and it also depends upon the purpose of the analysis. The language of harmony is full of subtleties, and there are few passages in music which are not open to a variety of interpretations.

(No response.)

7.60   There is an intimate relationship between harmonic progression and the phrase. An examination of this relationship will shed additional light upon the way chords are related, and will prepare for the technique of harmonizarion which is the subject of Chapter 8.0.

The harmony of the phrase is dominated by the CADENCE; it is the focal point — the "point of arrival" — toward which the melodic contour, rhythm, and harmony are directed.

The focal point of the phrase is the _____.

cadence

7.61   Although phrases seemingly may be harmonized in an infinite number of ways, a few simple practices are the most prevalent. These involve the extent to which the cadence formula dominates the phrase, and how the harmony leads into the cadence itself.

We shall observe three types of phrases:

1.   Phrases built on a single chord followed by a cadence.

2.   Phrases with harmonic embellishment of a single chord followed by a cadence.

3.   Phrases in which a basic progression is spread over the entire phrase.

Harmonic progression is related to the structure of the

_____.

phrase

■ 7.62 The example below shows a phrase which is built on a single chord (the tonic) followed by a cadence.

Verdi, *La Traviata*, Act III, No. 16

Cadence

With what type of cadence does the above example close?

(Authentic/Plagal/ Half/Deceptive) _____

Authentic.

■ 7.63 Another example of a phrase which is built on a single chord followed by a cadence is shown on the next page.

Mozart, *Quartet*, K. 387

Andante cantabile

C: I

Authentic.

What type of cadence is used to close the pharse?_____

Embellishing.

7.64   The example below shows harmonic embellishment of the tonic followed by a cadence.

Haydn, *Capriccio*

Moderato

G: I   (V) I   (V) I   ii⁶ I⁶₄ V   I

$$\text{G:} \quad \text{I} \quad \text{(V)} \ \text{I} \quad \text{(V)} \ \text{I} \quad \text{ii}^{6} \ \text{I}^{6}_{4} \ \text{V} \quad \text{I}$$

Tonic Embellished   Cadence
                                 Formula

Are the dominant chords in the second and third measures

examples of structural or embellishing harmony? _____

7.65 A simple harmonic formula (I-IV-V-I) supplies the basis for the entire phrase in the example below. Note that the chords are spaced evenly throughout the phrase.

Boccherini, *Concerto for 'Cello in B-flat Major*

In this phrase only (primary/secondary) _____ triads are used.

primary

7.66 Phrases based on the harmonic formula shown in the preceding frame (I-IV-V-I) are very numerous in the music of the classical period. Through chord substitution and harmonic embellishment, however, considerable variety can be achieved. In the example on the next page, the supertonic triad is substituted for the subdoninant (measure 2), and the submediant triad is used as incidental harmony in the first measure.

Mozart, *Sonata*, K. 333

Variants of the progression I-IV-V-I often serve as the harmonic

phrase

basis for an entire _____

7.67   The harmonic basis of the phrase below is I-IV-V.

Mendelssohn, *Six Pieces for Children*, Op. 72, No. 3

(No response.)

The several chords which are indicated by the bracket above the staff do not serve a structural function; they appear more or less incidentally between those chords which provide the structural harmonic basis for the phrase.

Summary

One of the variable factors in harmonic progression is the relation of the basic harmonic structure to the phrase as a whole. Three types of harmonic structure have been shown: phrases built on a single chord (usually the tonic) followed by a cadence, phrase with harmonic embellishment of a single chord followed by a cadence, and phrases in which a harmonic progression (such as I-IV-V-I) serves as the basis for the entire phrase.

But you must not think that all phrases fall into one of these three types. The harmonic element of music is subtle and the effect of chord relations is unpredictable. Harmonies are selected for their affective value, and the response they elicit eludes simple rationalization. Also, music resists being ordered into neat patterns of analysis; an approach which serves well for one period or composer may be useless for another. The information contained in this chapter is merely an introduction — the study of harmonic progression continues in the next chapter. Your sensitivity to the language of harmony will increase not only by study and practice, but also through your performing and listening experiences.

Some other helpful hints *(observations)*:

1. The leading tone triad (vii°) is generally not used in root position in either a major or minor key.

2. The diminished supertonic (ii°) is also not generally used in root position in minor.

3. In general, iii probably resolves better to vi than to I, although both are technically "progressions."

4. The following chord progression should probably be used with caution and within certain limited musical contexts:

$$\text{vii}_6 \text{ - I or } \text{I}_6; \quad \text{or} \quad \text{vii}°_6 \text{ - } \text{i}_6$$

$$\text{ii}_6 \text{ - V}; \quad \text{or} \quad \text{ii}°_6 \text{ - V}$$

5. The constitution of a "good" progression is ultimately a matter of personal taste reconciled with musical style. One will find many times that theory instructors simply will never totally agree on these things, so it is necessary in the final analysis — pardon the pun — to find one's own way.

Mastery Frames

	Up	Down
Fifths		√
Seconds	√	
Thirds		√

(7.20–.25)

7–1   Check (√) the root movements that result in progressions.

Root Movement	Up	Down
Fifths	_____	_____
Seconds	_____	_____
Thirds	_____	_____

---

(1)   fifth

(2)   sixth

(3)   seventh

(7.6–.9)

7–2   Complete each statement.

(1)   Root movement up a fourth is the same as down a

_____

(2)   Root movement down a third is the same as up a

_____

(3)   Root movement up a second is the same as sown a

_____

True.

(7.29–.32)

7–3   Root movement from the tonic to any other triad is

progressive. (True/False) _____

Secondary Triads

Submediant

Supertonic

Mediant, Leading tone

(7.35–.47)

7–4   Give the proper names of the secondary triad(s) related to each pormary triad.

Primary Triads	Secondary Triads
Tonic	_____
Subdominant	_____
Dominant	_____

Progressive. (7.36–.38)	7–5 Is movement from a primary triad to its secondary triad progressive or retrogressive? _____
structural (7.50–.59)	7–6 Harmony that appears at important points in the phrase such as at cadences is called _____ harmony.
Embellishment of a single chord (I) followed by a cadence. (7.64)	7–7 Describe the harmonic structure of the phrase below. _____ _____ C:

Supplementary Assignments

ASSIGNMENTS 7-1   Name_____

1. Indicate the root movement in each case. Use the signs ↓5, ↑5, ↓2, ↑2, ↓3, and ↑3. *(Be alert for inversions.)*

2. Classify each root movement in question 1 as either a *progression* (P) or a *retrogression* (R).
    Remember: harmonic movement away from the tonic is *progressive* in all cases.

    1 _____   3 _____   5 _____   7 _____   9 _____

    2 _____   4 _____   6 _____   8 _____   10 _____

3. For each of the primary triads below write the secondary triad(s) to which they relate. Use correct part writing procedures and provide the Roman numeral analysis.

(1) Tonic   (2) Subdominant   (3) Dominant

                                                        (a)   (b)

C: I   ___   IV   ___   V   ___   ___

4. Indicate each case below as either *progressive* (P) or *retrogressive* (R).

    (1) Movement from a primary triad to its secondary triad(s)._____

    (2) Movement from a secondary triad to its primary triad. _____

5. Classify each of the harmonic movements below as a progression or retrogression.

    V-vi   _____

    I-vii°   _____

    IV-iii   _____

    iii-V   _____

6. The deceptive cadence is an example of a secondary triad substituted for its primary triad.

    (True/False) _____

7. Which example demonstrates movement from a primary triad to its seondary triad? ____

    (1)   (2)   (3)

    E♭:

8. Explain, in your own words, the distinction between structural and embellishing harmony.

    _____

    _____

ASSIGNMENT 7–2   Name _____

1. Classify each of the harmonic movements below as a progression or retrogression.

      vii°-vi   _____

      iii-IV   _____

      ii-V   _____

      IV-vii°   _____

      I-iii   _____

2. Revise the progression below to show substitution of secondary triads for primary triads.

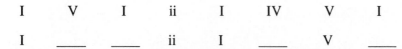

    I   V   I   ii   I   IV   V   I

    I   ___   ___   ii   I   ___   V   ___

3. Which example demonstrates substitution of a secondary triad for its primary triad? ____

e:

4. Compose a phrase for piano based on the given harmonic structure. Choose your own key and meter. Piano styles 2-12 are recommended (see Appendex B).

5. Describe the harmonic structure of the phrase above._____

_____

_____

6. Compose two phrases for piano based on the harmonic structures given below. Keys are given, but you may choose your own meters. Notate completely, including tempo, dymanics and phrasing indications. Piano styles 13-18 for Example A and 19-25 for Example B are recommended.

7. Describe the harmonic structure of the phrases above. _____

_____

_____

8. Compose a short work for piano which embodies the features below:

    (1) At least four phrases

    (2) Each phrase should be based on one of the harmonic structures below:

         (a) A single chord followed by a cadence
         (b) A single chord embellished, followed by a cadence
         (c) A harmonic progression spread evenly over the entire phrase

    (3) Key and meter of your choice

    (4) Piano style of your choice

    (5) Complete notation (tempo, dynamic and phrasing indications).

Chapter 8.0
The Technique of Harmonization

The harmonization of a melody involves selecting those chords from the available tonal material that realize the melody's harmonic implications. Even very simple melodies suggest more than one harmonization, so it is not a question of finding the "right" solution, but of selecting one of the alternatives that is stylistically consistent and appropriate to the function of the melody in the composition as a whole. You are not expected to learn to harmonize just like Bach, Mozart or Schubert even though music by these and other composers is used to illustrate various points throughout the book. You are learning a "technique" of harmonization, not a specific harmonic style. The lesson of this chapter should lead to the development of your own mode of harmonic expression.

8.1 Our study of the technique of harmonization is based upon the tonal material which has been presented to this point. We are limited, therefore, to the triads of a single tonality; but these may be used in first and second inversions as well as in root position. The technique learned in terms of this limited material will be equally valid when additionl resources become available.

The melody below will be used to demonstrate the technique of harmonization.

Sing (or play) this melody to become familiar with its characteristics.

E-flat

This melody is in the key of _____major.

8.2 You have just performed the first step in harmonizing a melody: become familiar with its characteristics and identifying its tonality. Next you must select an appropriate cadence. The last two notes of this melody suggest two cadences as shown with Roman numerals.

KEY OF E-FLAT MAJOR

Cadences: { 1. V   I
             2. V   vi

Authentic

Deceptive

Name these cadences.

Cadence No. 1 _____

Cadence No. 2 _____

8.3   Melodies often suggest more than one type of cadence. It is important to decide on the cadence which is appropriate for the end of a particular phrase.

Play the melody and try each of the two cadences as notated below:

Which cadence gives the stronger sense of finality? (1) or (2)

(1).

_____

8.4   This demonstration involves only a single phrase, so we shall choose the authentic cadence for its stronger closing effect. The deceptive cadence would imply another phrase to carry forward and complete the musical idea of the first phrase. Contrasting cadences are highly desirable, so they should be chosen with care.
    The choice of cadence is dictated entirely by the contour of the

False.
(The degree of finality desired is important.)

melody. (True/False) _____

8.5   The cadence has a strong influence upon the harmonies which precede it. The harmonic destination must be known before you can select the chords which will take you there. This is why it is so important to choose the cadence before starting to harmonize the first part of the melody.
    The harmony of a phrase is strongly infuenced by the_____

cadence

_____.

harmonic rhythm	8.6 The rate at which harmony changes, or, more succinctly, chord changes, is referred to as HARMONIC RHYTHM. Harmonic rhythm contributes to the motivation of music and plays an important expressive role. Some passages are based on slow changes of harmony, others feature very rapid changes, still others have varying rates of harmonic changes which increase the rhythmic complexity of the composition. The temporal element of harmony is called_____.
True.	8.7 Returning to the melody which we are using to demonstrate the technique of harmonization, it is desirable at this point to settle upon an appropriate harmonic rhythm. The prevailing quarter-note rhythm of the melody suggests the same rhythm for the harmony. This is not the only possibility, for either one or two chords per measure could be employed to good effect. The limited material at our disposal. however, rules out these choices since not all of the melodic notes could be included in such a harmonic scheme. Most melodies give rise to several possibilities of harmonic rhythm. (True/False) _____.
chord	8.8 In completing the harmonization of the melody, the prevailing rate of chord change will be the quarter note. Two notes separated by a leap and from a strong to a weak beat are frequently harmonized by the same chord. The first two notes (G and B-flat), for example, are both members of the tonic triad. Since it is desirable to begin a phrase with tonic emphasis, it makes good sense to use the tonic triad for these two notes. Our harmonization now stands as below: Eb: I I V I Melodic leaps often give a clue to effective chord choice. The two tones of a melodic leap from a strong to a weak beat often are harmonized by the same_____.

(No response.)	8.9 Let us review the steps we have taken to arrive at this point. We have (1) determined the tonality (E-flat major), (2) chosen an appropriate cadence (authentic), (3) chosen an appropriate harmonic rhythm (principally in quarter-note rhythm), and (4) begun the harmonic phrase with tonic emphasis (suggested by the notes G and B-flat, both of which are members of the tonic triad).

8.10   Now play the phrase with the chords which already have been selected.

Three types of harmonic phrase structure were discussed in Chapter 7.0: (1) phrase consisting of a single chord followed by a cadence, (2) phrases consisting of the tonic embellished followed by a cadence, and (3) phrases based upon a harmonic formula such as I-IV-V-I.*

Your ear and imagination must be brought into play to decide which of these patterns is best suited to this melody.

Melodies usually are not harmonized by selecting a chord more or less independently for each successive note. The final choice evolves slowly, as a result of careful reference to the cadence and

phrase *(or melody)*

to the _____ as a whole.

_____

*You may wish to review Chapter 7.0, especially Frames 7.61–.67

8.11   Since the fourth scale degree (A-flat) is stressed by appearing on both the first and second beats of the second measure, a subdominant emphasis is appropriate for these notes.

Play the phrase with the additions below:

By now it is clear that the phrase is based on one of the simple harmonic formulas. Write the formula in Roman numerals.

I-IV-V-I

_____

8.12   Having come this far, and with only three notes yet to be harmonized, your ear should help you complete the harmonization. As an aid in making these final few choices, however, you may wish to list the possibilities for each note.

Since the tonal material is limited to triads, a given note can be harmonized by one of three triads. For example, the third note of the melody (C) may be the root of the submediant triad (CE♭ G), the third of the subdominant triad (A♭ CE♭), or the fifth of the supertonic triad (FA♭ C). Applying this method to the other remaining notes, the chords from which your may choose to complete the harmonization are listed below:

E: I - vi   V   IV - iii   V   I
                IV   iii   I
                ii   I   vi

When the tonal material is limited to triads, any note may be harmonized by one of three triads, The note may be either the

root, third, (or) fifth
(Any order.)

_____, _____, or _____ of a triad.

8.13   The choice between the alternatives listed in the preceding frame is influenced by the balance between progressive and retrogressive harmonic movement which is desired, and also by practical necessities of part writing which may not be revealed until later. But the final choice is based largely upon personal preference. *The basic underlying progression will hold the phrase together regardless of the decisions which are made at this point.*

The chords which will be used in this demonstration are shown below:

E♭:   I - vi iii   IV - I   V   I

Although some choices may produce more effective results than others, the harmonic structure which practically guarantees the stability of this phrase consists of the progression

I-IV-V-I

(Roman numerals)_____.

8.14   It is vital that the bass be an effective melodic line which complements the soprano. The use of some contrary motion between the soprano and bass is desirable as it gives each a measure of independence. The other voices (soprano and bass) define the "vertical" limits of music, and individuality in these voices contributes greatly to the musical interest.

Compare the soprano and bass of our harmonization as it now stands.

Eb: I - vi iii   IV - I V   I

Evaluate each item.

1.   Melodic contour of the bass. (Good/Fair/Poor) _____
2.   Effectiveness of the bass in relation to the soprano (Good/

Your opinion.

Fair/Poor) _____

8.15   Regardless how you rated the bass in the preceding frame, it can be improved as a melodic line by eliminating some of the large leaps. The bass usually contains a greater number of leaps than the other voices; but, even so, the angularity in the second measure is not especially good.

Observe the changes below:

Eb: I - vi iii   IV ii I$^6_4$ V   I

Two changes have been made: at (1) the supertonic has been substituted for its primary triad (the subdominant), and at (2) the tonic triad has been placed in second inversion. The cadence for-

cadential

mula now includes the use of a _____ six-four chord.

8.16 Though slight, these changes bring greater tonal variety to the passage, reduce the angularity of the bass, and avoid the monotonous repetition of A-flat in both the soprano and bass simultaneously (beats one and two of the second measure, Frame 8.14).

    Substitution of secondary for primary triads, and the use of inver-

bass

sions, helps refine the quality of the _____line.

8.17 You should check the soprano and bass voices against one another for incorrect use of parallel motion. Such errors are easier to detect before the alto and tenor voices are written.

    Indicate the type of motion in the spaces provided. Use the following abbreviations: O = oblique, C = contrary, S = similar; P = parallel.

O C S C O C O C

No.
(Parallel thirds and sixths are good.)

8.18 Since no parallal motion occurs between the soprano and bass, the possibility of incorrect parallel motion does not exist. Is all

parallel motion between the soprano and bass forbidden? _____

8.19 The melodic quality of the bass line and its relation to the soprano is important, as much of the success of the harmoninzation depends upon a good bass. An effective bass possesses the following features:

1. *Melodic contour.* The bass line should not be too angular even though more leaps are to be expected than in the upper parts.

2. *Contrapuntal interest with the soprano.* The bass and soprano together should make effective two-part writing — some contrary motion is desirable.

3. *Tonal variety.* Inversions help provide a more melodic bass line and contribute to tonal variety.

(No response.)

4. *Parallel motion.* Always check for parallel fifths and octaves between the bass and soprano before writing the remaining voices.

8.20 Complete the harmonization by writing the alto and tenor voices.

(Use close structure.)

8.21 You should have had no trouble completing the harmonization as the alto and tenor voices fall neatly into place. Sometimes, however, part writing problems arise which can not be solved. When this happens, changes in the bass line, such as the use of different inversions, or even the selection of new chords, will be necessary. Even with only the limited hamonic material with which we are working there are many ways a melody can be harmonized. So do not be reluctant to substitute one chord for another no matter how enamored you are of your first choice.

Part writing difficulties sometimes are solved by the selection of

a different chord, or by the use of _____.

inversions

8.22 We have completed one demonstration of the technique of harmonization. Before trying another, let us review briefly the principal steps taken:

1. Determine the tonality.

2. Choose an appropriate cadence,

3. Choose an appropriate harmonic rhythm.

4. Determine the basic harmonic structure of the phrase. (Look for notes which are emphasized by prolongation, contour, or rhythm.)

5. Select chords for notes which remain from the three possibilities for each.

6. Write the bass.

7. Write the alto and tenor.

8. Make adjustments if necessary.

(No response.)

	8.23 Check (√) the correct option: 1. Harmonic rhythm is always identical with the rhythm of the melody. 2. In four-part writing the bass is a melodic line nearly equal in importance to the soprano. True statements: (1) _____ (2) _____ Both _____ Neither _____
(2) √	
B minor.	8.24 We shall continue with another demonstration of the technique of harmonization, What is the tonality of the melody below? _____. Cruger, Chorale: *Herzliebster Jesu, was hast du verbrochen*
Half cadence. *(See next frame.)*	8.25 Notice that the melody in the preceding frame does not end on the key note. What cadence is suggested by this phrase? _____
i-V, VI-V, or III-V	8.26 The melody in Frame 8.24 ends with the second scale degree. This note is not included in the tonic or submediant chords, so authentic, plagal and deceptive cadences are not possible. The half cadence is the only one possible in this case. Show with Roman numerals two chords which produce a half cadence. _____ _____

The tonic (i).	8.27 The final dominant chord can be preceded by i, VI, or III. You may try these three possibilities at the piano to acquaint yourself with the effect of each.
	       Under proper circumstances any one of these possibilities might be effective. The combination III-V, however, is probably the weakest, because in this case a primary triad (V) is preceded by its secondary triad (III). Our choice shall be i-V.
	       With what chord would you expect the harmonization to begin?
	
	_____

8.28   The harmonization now has a beginning and an ending.

The cadence we have selected is a (final/nonfinal)

nonfinal

_____cadence.

8.29   Does the melody suggest a harmonic rhythm of the whole

The quarter note.

note, half note or quarter note? _____

8.30   Now sing (or play) the melody, which is notated again below. Notice particularly the tones which suggest tonic harmony.
    Draw a circle around each of the notes which could be harmon-
ized with the tonic chord.

8.31   It is evident there is a strong tonic emphasis in this melody.
This suggests that the basic harmonic structure of the phrase
should be tonic (embellished) followed by a

cadence

_____.

8.32   Let us write the tonic triad wherever it may be used.

Play the phrase as it now stands.

Do you find the effect of so many tonic triads to be rather

monotonous? _____

Yes.
(There should be little disagreement.)

8.33   The prevalence of implied tonic harmony was shown in the preceding frame to make clear the underlying harmonic design of this melody. Represented by Roman numerals this is simply:

i ——————————————→ _____
                            ↑

(Write the appropriate Roman numeral here.)

V

8.34   The tonic triad need not be used as often as suggested in Frame 8.32. Some substitutions can be made and additional tonal variety can be obtained by the use of inversions. *But it is important to recognize the basic harmonic implications of a melody early in the processes of harmonization.*

Tonic harmony should be avoided except at the beginning and end

of the phrase. (True/False) _____

False.
(Tonic harmony may occur at any point in the phrase.)

8.35   Let us proceed now to the selection of chords for those notes yet to be harmonized. Since each note may be the root, third, or fifth of a triad, there are three possibilities. The choices which exist for the first two of the remaining notes are shown below. Indicate the choices for the third remaining note (E).

iv
ii°
vii°

(Any order.)

b: i   i   i   V   i

i   vii°6   i   i

iv   i   V

8.36   The choice between these possibilities is influenced by the changes we make in the tonic harmonies. It is at this point that your sense of style and creative imagination must be brought to bear.

To continue the demonstration, the chords shown in the Roman numeral analysis below will be used.

Complete the bass line in accordance with the Roman numeral given.

b: i   i   i   V   i   i vii°6 i i   iv   i   V

A diminished triad sounds best
in first inversion
(Or equivalent.)

8.37   There obviously is room for much improvement, both in the choice of chords and in the quality of the bass line. But don't expect a harmonization to take shape instantly; it usually develops slowly with the final product the result of much experimentation and compromise.

Why is it necessary to place the chord at the asterisk in first

inversion? _____

8.38   Now follow the steps which are taken to refine the bass line and the choice of chords. We wish to eliminate some of the tonic triads by substituting other chords and also provide greater tonal variety by the use of inversions. At the beginning of the phrase it would be desirable to have harmonic change to counter the monotony of the repeated notes in the soprano.

Two possibilities are shown below:

b: i   iv i6 V   i   VI iv   V

inversions.

Repeated notes in the melody often call for harmonic changes

or the use of _____.

8.39 We shall choose possibility No.1 of the preceding frame. So now our harmonization looks like this:

At the asterisk, the repetition of the tonic chord from the fourth beat of the first measure to the first beat of the second measure produces harmonic stagation. It is usually desirable to have harmonic motion at a point of metric stress (such as the first beat of a measure), so some change is needed. What two chords other than the tonic can be used to harmonize the F-sharp?

(Use Roman numerals.) _____ and _____.

V (and) III+

8.40 Since the leap from A-sharp to F-sharp at the asterisk defines the dominant triad, a repetition of this harmony on the fourth beat is also appropriate. By using the following tonic chord in first inversion the parallel octaves (B to C-sharp) are eliminated.

Incorrect use of parallel motion often is prevented by the use of

inversions

_____.

8.41   Now the first part of the harmonization has been greatly improved. One additional change which will add interest to the latter part is shown at the asterisk below:

The submediant triad (VI) may often be substituted for the tonic

secondary

because it is the tonic's _____ triad.

8.41   Now that all of the chords have been chosen, it is necessary to examine the bass line and its relation to the soprano.
      Evaluate the bass as written in the preceding frame.

1.   Is the bass a good melodic line? _____

1.   Your opinion

2.   Is there any incorrect parallel motion between the bass and soprano? _____

2.   No.

3.   Does the bass complement the soprano (is there effective use of contrary motion? _____

3.   Yes.

8.43   Write the alto and tenor voices.

The fifths are not both perfect. (A-sharp to E is a diminished fifth.) *(Or equivalent.)*	8.44 Notice in the solution given in the preceding frame that consecutive fifths occur in the second measure (beats two and three) between the alto and tenor voices. Why is this not an error?_____
perfect	8.45 Consecutive fifths are incorrect only if both intervals are _____.
(No response.)	8.46 An effective harmonization rarely appears instantly, but develops slowly and by successive stages. Compare, for example, our final version in the preceding frame with that of Frame 8.36. It is obvious that considerable improvement has taken place. Additional experience in harmonization will make it possible for you to proceed more quickly to the final version; *but until your technique becomes more highly developed, it would be unwise to omit any of the steps which are demonstrated in this chapter.*
1st 3 2nd 1 3rd 5 4th 7 5th 4 6th 2 7th 6 *(Unless all of your answers were correct review Frame 8.22.)*	8.47 Some of the steps which are associated with the process of harmonization are listed at the left below. Arrange these steps in proper sequence by writing the number of each step in the appropriate space at the right. 1. Choose an appropriate cadence. 2. Write the bass. 3. Determine the tonality. 4. Select chords for notes not associated with the basic harmonic structure. 5. Choose an appropriate harmonic rhythm. 6. Check for incorrect parallel motion between bass and soprano. 7. Determine the basic harmonic structure of the phrase. 1st _____ 2nd _____ 3rd _____ 4th _____ 5th _____ 6th _____ 7th _____
authentic	8.48 The choice of chords is influenced by the cadence, so do not begin to harmonize until the cadence has been selected. If the melody consists of several phrases, there should be variety in the types of cadences used. The final cadence, of course, should be the most conclusive. For this reason the final cadence usually is a perfect _____cadence.

8.49 For the remainder of this chapter you must draw on the knowledge you have acquired regarding effective chord choice and part writing procedures. Which chord ((a), (b), or (c)) most effectively continues the progression? _____

If your choice was:

(a) go to Frame 8.50

(b) go to Frame 8.51

(c) go to Frame 8.52

Bb: I   V   I   IV   vi   V   ii

(No response.)

8.50 The harmonic movement IV-vi is a retrogression (the bass moves up a third). While retrogressions are not entirely ruled out, there is a better choice. *Return to Frame 8.49 and try again.*

(No response.)

8.51 The progression IV-V is very strong, but the parallel fifths and octaves (between the bass and soprano, and between the bass and tenor) make this a poor choice. *Return to Frame 8.49 and try again.*

(No response.)

8.52 This is the best choice. The harmonic movement IV-ii is a progression (the root moves down a third), and the part writing is correct. *Proceed with the next frame.*

8.53 Which chord ((a), (b), or (c)) most effectively continues the progression? _____

If your choice was:

(a) go to Frame 8.54

(b) go to Frame 8.55

(c) go to Frame 8.56

c#:   iv   i$^6_4$ V   iv   VI   VI

(No response.)	**8.54** Several things are wrong with this choice. Not only is the harmonic movement V-iv weak, but there are parallel fifths between the bass and soprano. Notice, also, the incorrect doubling in the subdominant chord. *Return to Frame 8.53 and try again.*
deceptive *(Skip to Frame 8.57.)*	**8.55** This is the best choice. Notice that the third is doubled in the submediant triad. This is to avoid the augmented second which would have occurred if the tenor had taken an A (as in chord (c)). What type of cadence is illustrated in this example? A _____ cadence.
(No response.)	**8.56** The progression V-VI is good, but the augmented second between B-sharp and A in the tenor makes this a bad choice. *Return to Frame 8.53 to find a better solution.*
If your choice was: (a) go to Frame 8.58 (b) go to Frame 8.59 (c) go to Frame 8.60	**8.57** Which fragment ((a), (b), or (c)) most effectively continues the progression? _____
(No response.)	**8.58** The use of the leading tone triad (vii°) in root position makes this a poor choice. *Return to Frame 8.57 and try again.*
(No response.)	**8.59** The progression I-iii-IV-V-vi is a good one. Incorrect parallel motion between the second and third chords, however, makes this a bad choice. *Ruturn to Frame 8.57 and try again.*
Imperfect authentic.	**8.60** This is the best choice. Identify the type of cadence used. (*Be specific.*) _____

The final chord does not have the

keynote in the soprano.
(Or equivalent.)

8.61   Why is the cadence in Frame 8.57 (choice (c)) not

a perfect authentic cadence? _____

_____

_____

If your choice was:

(a)   go to Frame 8.64

(b)   go to Frame 8.63

8.62   Which fragment ((a) or (b)) most effectively continues

the progresseion? _____

(No response.)

8.63   The harmonic progression of (b) is a good one. There are, however, several flaws. The most serious of these is parallel octaves which occur between the second and third chords in the soprano and tenor voices (E to D). The bass line is exccessively angular; also, it is undesirable to leap too often in the bass from triads in first inversion. *Continue with the next frame to learn why (a) was the better choice.*

True.

8.64   You may have been reluctant to make this choice because of the retrogression V-IV. Retrogressions, however, often provide good harmonic interest, and you should not be afraid to use them if good voice leading results.

You may refer to Frame 8.63 to learn why (b) is weak.

If not used to excess, retrogressions are equal in

effectiveness to progressions. (True/False) _____

Weaken.

8.65   There should be an appropriate balance between progressions and retrogressions. This balance fluctuates drastically depending upon the wishes of the composer at a given moment. Merely as an arbitrary norm for an appropriate balance, let us suggest two-thirds progression and one-third retrogression as reasonable.

Does an excess of retrogressive harmonic relationships weaken or strengthen the sense of forward motion? _____

If your choice was:

(a)   go to Frame 8.67

(b)   go to Frame 8.68

8.66   Which fragment ((a) or (b)) most effectively continues the progression? _____

(No response.)

8.67   There is actually nothing wrong with either (a) or (b). This example is given to show that there are more ways than one to harmonize even a simple melodic line. The choice between these two possibilities is one of personal preference, as well as the type of cadence desired. Continue with Frame 8.68 for a comment on choice (b).

(No response.)

8.68   Although there is nothing wrong with this choice, many of you may prefer (a). The reason is that in (b) the dominant chord (V) is used on both the second and third beats immediately prior to the cadence chord. This reiteration of dominant harmony results in a stagnation of the harmonic rhythm. The greater sense of motion which results from the progresseion ii-V in (a) is desirable.

   Read the comments in Frame 8.67 before continuing with Frame 8.69.

---

(2) √

8.69   Check (√) the correct option:

1.   Structural harmony occurs only at cadence points.
2.   Relatively rapid chord changes produce animated harmonic rhythm.

True statements:

(1) _____   (2) _____   Both _____   Neither _____

Summary

The finished harmonization evolves from an assessment of the basic harmonic implications of the melody. Structural harmony — chords which constitute the tonal framework of the phrase — should be chosen first. Remember that tonal stability and modal clarity result chiefly from the use of primary triads in important structural positions. If used to excess, secondary triads weaken the tonality.

The steps to harmonizing a melody that are presented in this chapter are summarized below:

1. Familiarize yourself with the melody by singing or playing it.

2. Determine the key to be used. Some melodies may be harmonized in more than one key.

3. Select an appropriate cadence. If the phrase is one of a group of phrases, cadences should complement one another.

4. Choose an appropriate harmonic rhythm. The melody may suggest a particular rate of chord change, such as one or two per measure, or perhaps call for a chord for each note.

5. Determine the basic harmonic structure of the phrase. The three sturctures that have been presented are:

    a. A single chord followed by a cadence.

    b. Harmonic embellishment of a single chord followed by a cadence.

    c. A cadence formula (or a basic harmonic progression such as I-IV-V-I) spread over the entire phrase.

6. Select the remaining chords. Any note may be the root, third, or fifth of a triad. Progressions should predominate over retrogressions.

7. Write the bass voice. Produce an effective melodic line by using first and second inversions when appropriate. The bass should complement the melody. A variety of relative motion is desirable. Contrary motion contributes to the individuality of voices.

8. Check for incorrect parallel motion between the bass and soprano voices.

9. Write the alto and tenor voices. Each should produce an agreeable melodic line.

10. Check for part writing errors, including incorrect doubling, spacing and parallel perfect intervals.

Mastery Frames

8–1   Check (√) the cadence(s) that would be appropriate for the melody below:

G:

(1)   Authentic _____   (3)   Half _____

(2)   Plagal _____   (4)   Deceptive _____

(3) √

(7.64–.67; 8.1–.5)

8–2   Check (√) the cadence(s) that would be appropriate for the melody below:

c:

(1)   Authentic _____   (3)   Half _____

(2)   Plagal _____   (4)   Deceptive _____

(1)   Authentic √

(4)   Deceptive √

(7.64–.67; 8.1–.5)

8–3   Circle the notes that could be harmonized with the tonic triad.

F:

(2).

8–4   Which harmonic phrase structure is suggested by

the melody in the preceding frame? _____

(1)   A single chord followed by a cadence.

(2)   The tonic embellished followed by a cadence.

(3)   A harmonic formula spread over the entire phrase.

(8.10)

8–5   Indicate with Roman numerals the three triads that might be
used at (1) and (2).

(1)	(2)
IV	ii
ii	vii°
vii°	V

(8.12)

Supplementary Assignments

ASSIGNMENT 8–1   Name _____

1. Write chord symbols and identify the cadences that are appropriate for the melodic lines.

CADENCE TYPE

(A) C: ___ ___   _____

     ___ ___   _____

(B) Ab: ___ ___   _____

(C) g: ___ ___   _____

(D) c#: ___ ___   _____

(E) G: ___ ___   _____

2. Check (√) the note value of the prevalent harmonic rhythm suggested by each of the melodies below.

3. The three chords provided in the example below indicate the basic harmonic structure of the phrase. Complete the harmonization by selecting chords for the remaining notes of the melody that produce mostly progressive harmonic movement. Use inversions and employ correct part writing procedures.

4. Complete the harmonization and supply the Roman numeral analysis.

The Technique of Harmonization

ASSIGNMENT 8–2   Name _____

1. Show with Roman numerals the three triads that may be used to harmonize each note of the major scale.

2. Show with Roman numerals the three triads that may be used to harmonize each note of the minor scale.

3. Complete the harmonization and supply the chord symbols.

4. Harmonize the melodies below using the method that is summarized in Frame 8.22.
    Analyze with Roman numerals.

G:

a:

f:

A:

Chapter 9.0
Nonharmonic Tones

The tones of a musical composition belong to one of two groups: *harmonic tones* — those which constitute chords; and *nonharmonic tones* — those which are extraneous to the harmony. If all tones were harmonic, music would be excessively consonant. Although not all nonharmonic tones are dissonant, most are, and motivation results from the dissonant tensions they produce. Nonharmonic tones also contribute to smoother melodic lines and greater rhythmic animation.

■ 9.1 Most music contains many tones which are not included in the harmony. These are called NONHARMONIC TONES.

Since the note C is not part of the chord which is sounding at the

moment it appears, it is called a _____ tone.

nonharmonic

■ 9.2 Whether or not a note is called a nonharmonic tone sometimes depends upon the analysis. *Not all nonharmonic tones are dissonant.*

In (1) the note E is called a nonharmonic tone because it is not part of the harmony as it is analyzed. In (2), however, two chords (ii and vii°⁶) are analyzed on the second beat; this causes both the E and F-sharp to be included in the harmony.

Any tone which is not part of the harmony as it is analyzed is

True.

called a nonharmonic tone. (True/False) _____

9.3   Nonharmonic tones originate in the melodic and rhythmic aspects of music. Melodies often contain a greater number of notes than can be accommodated by the harmony. Occasionally very rapid harmonic rhythm is used to harmonize each note of a melody, but such practice becomes tiresome if carried on too long.

Schumann, *Symphonic Studies*, Op. 13

All of the notes in the above example are included in the harmony; thus, in spite of very rapid melodic movement, there are no nonharmonic tones.

Rapid harmonic rhythm tends to reduce the number of nonhar-

True.

monic tones. (True/False) _____

9.4   The harmonic rhythm of the following example is much slower than that shown in the preceding frame. The circled notes are not included in the harmony.

Beethoven, *Sonata for Violin and Piano*, Op. 24

F: I

vi   ii

Music which has slow harmonic rhythm tends to contain (few/

many _____ nonharmonic tones; however, musical
examples can also be found with slow harmonic rhythm and many
harmonic-only tones.

many

9.5   Nonharmonic tones contribute to the smoothness of melodic
lines by reducing the number of leaps. They also increase the rhythmic activity. By staggering rhythmic activity in each of the voices,
greater individuality results.

Each voice has little individuality in the example below as the
rhythm is the same for each.

Bach, Chorale: *Ach Gott, wie manches Herzeleid*
(altered)

No.	Are there any nonharmonic tones in the above example? _____

■   9.6   Compare the example below with that in the preceding frame.

Bach, Chorale: *Ach Gott, wie manches Herzeleid*

Certainly you will agree that the example above (with nonharmonic tones) is much more interesting than the version in the preceding frame. Each voice receives greater individuality through

nonharmonic | the use of _____tones.

No.
(Melodies without leaps are monotonous and quite rare.)

9.7   In addition to greater individuality through rhythmic activity, each voice (Frame 9.6) is a better melodic line. Nonharmonic tones reduce the number of leaps and give the music a more "flowing" quality.
   Is it desirable for melodic lines to be entirely free of leaps?_____

(No response.)

9.8   The use of nonharmonic tones often causes irregularities of doubling or in the distribution of the voices. Refer again to Frame 9.5. In the third chord the alto is below the tenor. There would be no reason to cross the voices in this fashion if no nonharmonic tones were employed. Frame 9.6, however, shows why this is desirable. The momentum of the ascending scale line in the tenor carries it up to the note E, and the alto drops down to A to improve the sonority of the chord. Normal distribution of the voices is resumed in the fourth chord.
   In order to produce expressive melodic lines in each of the voices, irregularities of doubling or an occasional crossing of the voices is tolerated.

1, 5 (and) 7	9.9 In the example of Frame 9.6 there are three chords which contain irregular doubling. Indicate these chores (by number). _____, _____ and _____.
nonharmonic	9.10 In chord 1 (Frame 9.6) there are three roots and one third, but no fifth; chord 5 is in root position, so it would be normal to double the bass rather than the soprano as has been done here; chord 7 has two roots and two thirds, but no fifth. All of these irregularities result from the desire to write more expressive melodic lines through the use of _____tones.
(No response.)	9.11 While the use of nonharmonic tones permits greater freedom of part writing, not all of the "rules" are thrown to the wind. Nonharmonic tones normally do not justify the use of parallel fifths or octaves, nor is it desirable to double active tones (the leading tone, in particular). In fact, you will find that nonharmonic tones added to part writing which otherwise is correct often produce incorrect parallel motion so you must check more carefully than ever for such errors.
(2) √	9.12 Check (√) the correct option: 1. Nonharmonic tones must be analyzed as part of the harmony. 2. Nonharmonic tones give rhythmic interest to the voices. True statements. (1) _____ (2) _____ Both _____ Neither _____
Both √	9.13 Check (√) the correct option: 1. Nonharmonic tones often cause irregularities of doubling. 2. A tone which is not part of the harmony as analyzed is a nonharmoniuc tone. True statements. (1) _____ (2) _____ Both _____ Neither _____

9.14   There are several kinds of nonharmonic tones and the remainder of this chapter is devoted to naming them and learning to write them correctly. Unfortunately the terminology of nonharmonic tones is not standardized. Writers in the field of music theory often use different terms for the same device, or use the same term in conflicting ways. Even the term "nonharmonic tone" is not universal. Other terms are *accessory tone, bytone, nonchord tone* and *foreign tone*.

Actually, the name given to a particular nonharmonic tone is of little importance as long as its musical significance and correct interpretation are appreciated. Labels given to musical events are not an end in themselves; they make verbalization possible. Although standardization of terminology would be desirable, and communication greatly facilited, the fact remains that we must accommodate ourselves to different sets of terms when comparing the writings of various authors. You will find this is not difficult once an understanding of a particular device has been acquired.

Nonharmonic tones are usually classified according to the way they are approached and left. Further classification is made with reference to rhythmic placement.

(No response.)

9.15   A nonharmonic tone which is approached and left by step in the same direction is called a PASSING TONE (symbol: PT).

Schumann, *Album for the Young*, Op. 68, No. 11

Since the circled note (A) is not part of the harmony, it must be analyzed as a nonharmonic tone. It is called a passing tone be

cause it is approached and left by _____ in the same direction.

step

9.16   Passing tones may occur in either ascending or descending direction, and two or more may occur simultaneously.

In the following example there are nine passing tones; draw a circle around each. (*Refer to the Roman numeral analysis to identify the notes which are not part of the harmony.*)

Bach, Chorale: *Allein, zu dir, Herr Jesu Christ*

C: vi   I⁶   IV   I⁶   I   V

9.17   Notice in the preceding frame that when two or more passing tones occur simultaneously they produce consonant intervals with each other.

Passing tones may occur singly or in groups of two or more. All passing tones are approached and left by step in the same

direction   _____.

9.18   Figured bass symbols are used to indicate melodic movement over a single bass note.

In (1) the numbers 8 7 refer to the notes C and B which occur over the bass note C; in (2) the numbers 3 2 list the intervals between the bass and tenor (the actual intervals of a tenth and ninth are reduced to avoid the use of unnecessarily large numbers); the figuration in (3) is more complete to show the doubled third above the bass and the melodic movement in the soprano.

Numbers in the figured bass which occur *horizontally* beneath a single bass note indicate melodic movement in one of the upper voices.

(No response.)

9.19   Refer again to (3) in the preceding frame. Note that the dashes which follow the numbers 6 and 3 show that the notes indicated by these figures are held while melodic movement occurs in another voice.

Write the alto and tenor voices.

(1)   (2)   (3)

6   -   5 6   3 2
6   5   3 4   1 2

9.20   Write the alto and tenor voices.

8   7   8 9   5 6
             3 4

9.21   Write the alto and tenor voices. (*Note that the chord at the asterisk is a diminished triad — double accordingly.*

(In (3), the tenor may retain G.)

8   7   6 - 6   8 - 6
3   2   5 -
                           3 3

9.22   Examples (2) and (3) in the preceding frame show that when melodic movement occurs in the bass, dashes are used to indicate notes which are sustained while the bass moves. Complete the alto and tenor voices. (Remember: numbers in the figured bass represent intervals above the notes *under which the numbers occur.*)

(See next frame.)

The bass (3rd) should be doubled in a diminished triad in first inversion.

(In your own words.)

9.23   The second chord in (3) of the preceding frame is in first inversion. You may have doubled the soprano (B), but this is incorrect. State the reason why the soprano should *not* be doubled in this

chord. _____

_____

9.24   Draw a circle around each passing tone.

Bach, Chorale: *O Ewigkeit, du Donnerwort* *

F: I   I   vii°6   I6   I   IV   V   I

---

* Because of the wealth of excellent examples of nonharmonic tones in Bach's 371 Chorales, these will serve as the source for many of the exercises is this chapter.

9.25 Complete the alto and tenor voices and draw a circle around each passing tone.

Bach, Chorale: *Was mein Gott will, das g'scheh'*

```
8  7  5  6  5  -  6  -     6  5  4
      3  4  3  3  6  6     4  -  -
      3           -
```

9.26 All of the passing tones to this point have appeared on the weak portion of the beat. These are called UNACCENTED passing tones. Passing tones may also coincide with the strong portion of the beat, in which case they are called ACCENTED passing

(2).

tones. Which example shows an accented passing tone? _____

```
     (1)                    (2)

D:   I        I⁶    V    I        I⁶    V
```

9.27 Draw a circle around the *accented* passing tones. (*Refer to the Roman numeral analysis to find the notes which are not part of the harmony.*)

Bach, Chorale: *Helft mir Gott's Güte preisen*

```
a:  V⁶      i      i⁶    ii°⁶₅  V        I
```

9.28 Both of the accented passing tones in the preceding frame occur in descending motion. Although used most frequently in this fashion, accented passing tones may also occur in ascending motion.

Bach, Chorale: *Hast du denn, Jesu, dein Angesicht*

Bb: I   vii°6   I6   IV

The circled note (E) is nonharmonic with reference to the Roman numeral analysis. A different analysis for this beat (ii-vii°6) eliminates the nonharmonic tone. The analysis of nonharmonic tones must

take into account the _____ analysis.

harmonic

9.29 Sometimes two passing tones are used in succession. In this case the first is *unaccented* and the second is *accented*.

Bach, Chorale: *Du grosser Schmerzensmann*

G: vi   I6   IV   I6   vii°6   I

Single passing tones (either accented or unaccented) are used between two harmonic tones a third apart. Two passing tones in succession fill in the interval between two harmonic tones a

_____ apart.

fourth

9.30 Complete the alto and tenor voices in the following example, draw a circle around each passing tone and analyze.

Bach, Chorale: *Du grosser Schmerzensmann* (altered)

G: I vi I⁶ ii I⁶ V

5 -   5 - 5 -   6
         3 - 2 -
              2 -

G: __   __   __   __   __

D: I V IV⁶ V⁶ I

IV IV⁶ I

Both √

Neither √

9.31 Complete the alto and tenor voices, draw a circle around each passing tone and analyze.

Bach, Chorale: *Herzlich lieb hab' ich dich, o Herr* (altered)

5 6   5 6 6 5   6 - 5 -   5 - 6 -
       3 - 3 - 3 - 4 3
       3 -   3 6

D: __   __ __ __ __   __ __ __

9.32 Check (√) the correct option:

1. Passing tones are approached and left by step in the same direction.
2. Two or more passing tones may occur simultaneously.

True statements:

(1) _____   (2) _____   Both _____   Neither _____

9.33 Check (√) the correct option:

1. Passing tones occur only on weak portions of beats or measures.
2. It is not possible for two passing tones to occur in succession in the same voice.

True statements:

(1) _____   (2) _____   Both _____   Neither _____

9.34　A nonharmonic tone which is approached and left by step with a change of direction is called a NEIGHBORING TONE (symbol: NT).*

Beethoven, *Sonata*, Op. 49, No. 2

Whereas the passing tone leads by step from one harmonic note to another a third away, the neighboring tone appears between two

same

harmonic notes of the _____pitch

---
*Other terms for this device are *returning note*, *changing tone* and *auxiliary tone*.

9.35　Most neighboring tones occur on weak portions of beats or measures (as in the preceding frame). Accented neighboring tones, although less common, can sometimes be used effectively.

Chopin, *Valse Brillante*, Op. 34, No. 2

Neighboring tones may be either a step *above* or *below* the harmonic tone. Lower neighboring tones are shown in the first and third measures of the above example. Which measures contain upper

Two (and) four

neighboring tones? _____ and _____.

9.36 Frame 9.34 and 9.35 show that neighboring tones may be accented or unaccented, and occur (by step) either above or below the harmonic tone to which they relate.

Are most neighboring tones accented or unaccented?_____

Unaccented.

9.37 Draw a circle around each neighboring tone. *(Refer to the Roman numeral analysis.)*

Kuhlau, *Sonatine*, Op. 20, No. 1

C: I _____

9.38 Two or more neighboring tones may occur simultaneously. Draw a circle around the neighboring tones.

Bach, Chorale: *Herr, nun lass in Friede* (altered)

G: IV⁶ _____ V⁶₅ I   -

---

*For this chord, the pitch C is considered a chord tone. Chords with four different pitches (seventh chords) are discussed further in Chapters 10.0 and 11.0

9.39   Complete the alto and tenor voices and draw a circle around each neighboring tone; analyze.

Bach, Chorale: *Aus meines Herzens Grunde*

G: IV   ii(vii°⁶) I   V

$$\begin{array}{cccc} 8 & 7 & 9 & - \\ 3 & 2 & 4 & 6 \end{array}$$

G: __   __(__)__   __

---

passing tone

9.40   In the preceding frame, the second note in the bass voice (B) is a nonharmonic tone. It is an accented _____

9.41   Complete the alto and tenor voices and label each nonharmonic tone. *(Use the symbols PT and NT.)* Analyze.

Mendelssohn, Chorale: *Aus tiefer Noth schrei' ich zu dir*

Ab: IV   I⁶₄   V   I

$$\begin{array}{cccc} 5 & - & 8 & 7 \\ 5 & 6 & 6 & - 5 - \\ & & 4 & - 3 - \end{array}$$

Ab: __   __   __   __

9.42   A nonharmonic tone which is approached by leap and left by step (usually with a change of direction) is called as APPOGGIATURA (symbol: App).*

Beethoven, *Sonata*, Op. 10, No. 1

The feature which distinguishes the appoggiatura from both the passing tone and the neighboring tone is that it is approached

by_____.

_____

*The term appoggiatura comes from the Italian appoggiare, to lean. It describes the effect of this nonharmonic tone, which is that of "leaning" upon the tone to which it resolves. Some writers may also call accented passing and neighboring tones appoggiaturas.

leap

9.43   The appoggiatura occurs most often in a position of rhythmic stress (as in the preceding frame). The example below, however, shows *unaccented* appoggiaturas.*

Tchaikovsky, *Symphony No.* 5, Op. 64

Andante cantabile, con alcuna licenza

The appoggiatura is a nonharmonic tone which is approached

by leap and left by_____

_____

*Some writers may not agree that an appoggiatura can be unaccented.

step

9.44 Double appoggiaturas are shown in the example below.

Haydn, *Capriccio*
Moderato

G: I   ii⁶ I⁶₄ V I

Accented.

Are the appoggiaturas above accented or unaccented? _____

9.45 All of the appoggiaturas shown thus far have been approached by leap from *below*. They also may be approached from *above*.

Brahms, *Piano Concerto*, Op. 83
Allegretto

App

d: i   i⁶

V⁹   i

If an appoggiatura is approached from below, the note which follows is a step lower. If an appoggiatura is approached from above,

higher

the note which follows is a step _____.

9.46   The appoggiatura sometimes appears without preparation.

Bach, *French Suite No.* 3

With or without preparation, the appoggiatura is followed by a

step

tone which is a half- or whole- _____away.

9.47   Without prepatation, the appoggiatura's effect of "leaning" upon the harmonic tone which follows is heightened. The appoggiatura at the asterisk (next page) is an echo of that heard in the preceding measure. This produces a dramatic effect of emotional tension.

Tchaikovsky, *Romeo and Juliet*, *Overture-Fantasy*

poco a poco string. accel.

The appoggiaturas above are accented. Are the appoggiaturas in

Unaccented.

Frame 9.46 accented or unaccented? _____

9.48   Although the appoggiatura sometimes appears without preparation, it usually is approached by leap. In all cases it is left by step—usually in the direction opposite to its approach (if any). Some of the possible forms of the approggiatura are shown below:

WITH PREPARATION
(Accented)   (Unaccented)

WITHOUT PREPARATION
(Accented)   (Unaccented)

An appoggiatura which is approached from below will usually be

downward

left by step in a(n) (upward/downward)_____
direction.

Bb: I   I   vi   ii⁶   ii⁶   ii

I⁶₄   ii⁶   V   I

9.49   Complete the alto and tenor voices and label each nonharmonic tone. *(Use the symbols PT, NT, and App.)*

Bach, Chorale: *Jesu, nun sei gepreist*

Bb: __ __ __   __ __ __ __ __

9.50   A nonharmonic tone which is approached by step and left by leap (usually with a change of direction) is called an ESCAPE TONE (symbol: ET).*

Mozart, *Quartet*, K. 575

Allegretto

A: I   -   V⁷   I

The escape tone's melodic movement is the opposite of the appoggiatura's. Whereas the appoggiatura is approached by leap and left by step, the escape tone is approached by step and left by

leap   _____.

*The escape tone is also known by its French name *échappée*.

9.51   The most common form of the escape tone is shown in the preceding frame (an ascending step followed by a descending leap). The reverse form, however, is also used.

Franck, *Symphony in D Minor*

A nonharmonic tone which is approached by step and left by leap

escape tone   is called an _____.

9.52   Double escape tones are shown below:

Bach, Chorale: *Ach Gott, wie manches Herzeleid*

Escape tones which are approached from below are

downward   usually left (by leap) in a _____ direction.

9.53   Complete the alto and tenor voices in the following examples, label each nonharmonic tone and analyze.

G: I   IV   I   V   I

6 - 5 - 8 7
      3 4

G: ___ ___ ___ ___ ___

9.54   Complete the alto and tenor voices, label each nonharmonic tone and analyze.

Bach, Chorale: *Nicht so traurig, nicht so sehr* (altered)

c: i vii°⁶ i⁶ i V⁶ i   V

8 7   8 9 5 - 6   5 -
♮6 -   6 - 4 3   3 4   ♮

c: ___ ___ ___ ___ ___ ___

9.55   Complete the alto and tenor voices, label each nonharmonic tone and analyze.

Bach, Chorale: *Gott des Himmels und der Erden* (altered)

A: ii⁶₅   I⁶₄   V   I   I

6   6 7 8 -   8 7
5   4 5 3 7   5 4
                       3 2

A: ___   ___   ___   ___

(No response.)	9.56 The example in the preceding frame shows that several non-harmonic tones may occur simultaneously. Not only are there double escape tones, but also triple neighboring tones.

	9.57 Check (√) the type of nonharmonic tone shown in the example:
(3) √	(1) Accented passing tone _____ (4) Appoggiatura _____ (2) Unaccented passing tone _____ (5) Escape tone _____ (3) Neighboring tone _____ (6) None of these _____
	9.58 Check (√) the type of nonharmonic tone shown in the example:
(1) √	(1) Accented passing tone _____ (4) Appoggiatura _____ (2) Unaccented passing tone _____ (5) Escape tone _____ (3) Neighboring tone _____ (6) None of these _____
	9.59 Check (√) the type of nonharmonic tone shown in the example:
(4) √	(1) Accented passing tone _____ (4) Appoggiatura _____ (2) Unaccented passing tone _____ (5) Escape tone _____ (3) Neighboring tone _____ (6) None of these _____

9.60   Check (√) the type of nonharmonic tone shown in the example:

(6) √

(1) Accented passing tone _____   (4) Appoggiatura _____

(2) Unaccented passing tone _____   (5) Escape tone _____

(3) Neighboring tone   _____   (6) None of these _____

9.61   The nonharmonic tone in the preceding frame does not fall into any of the patterns presented thus far. It is approached by step and left by repetition. This type of nonharmonic tone is called an ANTICIPATION (symbol: A).

   The name of this nonharmopnic tone is an apt description of this musical function. It is a *premature* sounding of a harmonic tone to follow.

   The anticipation is always left by repetition of the same note.

(No response.)

9.62   The approach to the anticipation from *above* by step are shown:

Sibelius, *Finlandia*, Op. 26

Allegro

Ab: I$^6_4$ V^7 -   I

   The premature sounding of a hamonic tone that follows in the

anticipation   same voice, is called an _____.

■ 9.63 The anticipation may also be approached from below.

Handel, *Suite in D Minor*
Sarabande

d: i   iv⁶   V

Anticipations may be approached from above or below, and they usually occupy a relatively weak rhythmic position. They ordinarily are of shorter time value than the tone which is anticipated.

The anticipation is a premature sounding of a _____ tone.

harmonic
(or chord)

■ 9.64 Although most anticipations are approached by step, they are occasionally approached by leap.

Bach, *Well-Tempered Clavier*, Vol. 1, Prelude XIII

(Allegretto)

F#:   I   -   IV⁶

Regardless of the approach, the tone following the anticipation is always the _____ pitch.

same

9.65 Most anticipations occur as part of a cadence pattern over the dominant chord. It is usually the tonic note which is anticipated.

Handel, *Sonata No. 1 for Oboe and Harpsichord*

Anticipations may occur at any point in a phrase, but the

cadence

majority are found at the _____.

9.66 Check (√) the type of nonharmonic tone shown in the example:

(4) √

(1) Passing tone   _____   (4) Escape tone   _____

(2) Neighboring tone _____   (5) Anticipation   _____

(3) Appoggiatura   _____   (6) None of these _____

9.67 Check (√) the type of nonharmonic tone shown in the example:

(1) Passing tone   _____   (4) Escape tone _____

(2) Neighboring tone _____   (5) Anticipation _____

(3) Appoggiatura   _____   (6) None of these _____

(5) √

9.68 Check (√) the type of nonharmonic tone shown in the example:

(1) Passing tone   _____   (4) Escape tone _____

(2) Neighboring tone _____   (5) Anticipation _____

(3) Appoggiatura   _____   (6) None of these _____

(3) √

9.69 A nonharmonic tone which is approached by the same tone and left by step (upward or downward) is called a SUSPENSION (symbol: S). Both of the nonharmonic tones shown below meet these conditions.

F: I   V   V   I

The approach to a suspension is from a tone of the _____pitch.

same

step

9.70   The suspension is best understood as a figure composed of three parts; preparation, suspension and resolution. Whether the motion is upward or downward, the suspension proceeds to the

resolution by _____.

9.71   Label the three parts of each suspension figure. (P = Preparation, S = suspension and R = resolution.)

9.72   Check (√) the correct option:

1.   The suspension is prepared by a tone of the same pitch.

2.   The suspension may resolve to any tone (higher or lower).

True statements:

(1) _____   (2) _____   Both _____   Neither _____

(1) √
((2) is incorrect because the resolution must be by STEP.)

9.73   In most cases the preparation is sustained into the suspension by a tie or the note values used.

Continuous sounding (without repetition) of the preparation and suspension is considered by some to be an integral feature of the suspension. Current preference, however, is to classify nonharmonic tones according to the direction of movement preceding and following them. This approach simplifies terminology.

The preparation may be sustained into the suspension, or the

suspension may be re-sounded. (True/False) _____

True

9.74   Suspensions not tied to their preparation are shown below:

Suspensions such as these are sometimes called *appoggiaturas*. You must be prepared to accept alternate terms for several nonharmonic tones, as terminology is not standardized in this area of music theory.

(No response.)

■   9.75   Most suspension resolve DOWNWARD by step. Suspensions which resolve upward are relatively rare and sometimes are called RETARDATIONS.

Bach, *Well-Tempered Clavier*, Vol. 2, Prelude XII
(Moderato)

Since all of these suspensions are restruck, some theorists refer to them, as appoggiaturas. The suspensions at the asterisks resolve

retardation   upward. These are also known as _____.

9.76   Because suspensions are handled the same whether they resolve upward or downward, are sustained or re-sounded, it seems unnecessary to apply different terms in each case.

To summarize:

The suspension is a nonharmonic tone which is approached by the same pitch and left by step (usually downward). The preparation may be sustained (usually by tie) into the suspension, or the suspension may be re-sounded. The term *retardation* refers to a suspension which resolves upward.

(No response.)

■   9.77   We must now turn to a study of the rhythmic organization of the suspension figure.

Learn these principles:

1.   The suspension occurs on an accented portion of the measure (or beat).

2.   The resolution usually occurs on the weak beat (or portion of the beat) immediately following the suspension.

3.   The preparation is usually equal to or longer than the time value of the suspension.

The metric organization of the suspension figure is in accordance with either the unit or the division of the unit, and there is notable consistency within a composition once a rate has been established.

(1) UNIT RHYTHM   (2) DIVISION RHYTHM

8 7 6   6 - 4 3 3 6 7 6

In (1) the rhythmic value of the preparation is double that of the

No.

suspension. Is this true in each case in (2)? _____

9.78   The preparation often is twice as long as the suspension; but, as shown by the second suspension in example (2) of the preceding

equal

frame, it may also be _____ in value.

9.79   Whereas the preparation is usually equal to or longer than the time value of the suspension, this is not a binding rule. The example below shows a suspension whose preparation is six times as long.

Bach, *Well-Tempered Clavier*, Vol. 2, Fugue I
(Vivace)

Does the rhythmic movement of the suspension above coincide

The unit.

with the unit or with the division? _____

9.80   Below is an example of a suspension whose preparation is one-half as long.

Bach, *Well-Tempered Clavier*,
Vol. 2, Fugue XI
(Allegretto)

In all cases the resolution occupies a weaker rhythmic position

suspension

than does the _____.

9.81   *Types of suspensions.* Suspensions are classified according to the figured bass symbols which are appropriate to each. Thus we speak of 4-3, 7-6, 2-1 and 2-3* suspensions. These are shown in two-part writing below.

In a 7-6 suspension there is the interval of a seventh between the bass and suspension, and the interval of a sixth between the

resolution

bass and the _____.

Note that the 2-3 suspension occurs in the lowest part (see(5) above).

9.82   Write suspensions as directed by the figured bass.

9.83   Continue as in the preceding frame.

9.84   Continue as in the preceding frame.

9.85   Complete the alto and tenor voices and label each nonharmonic tone; analyze.

Bach, Chorale: *Wie schön leuchtet der Morgenstern*

9.86   Continue as in the preceding frame.

Bach, Chorale: *Befiehl du deine Wege*

9.87 The first suspension in the preceding frame is a 7-6 suspension. Of what type is the second? _____

4-3

9.88 Complete the alto and tenor voices, label each nonharmonic tone and analyze.

Bach, Chorale: *Es wird schier der letzte Tag herkommen*

$$\begin{matrix} 5 & - & 8 & - & 6 \\ 2 & - & 5 & - & \\ 2 & - & 3 & 4 & \end{matrix} \qquad \begin{matrix} 8 & 7 & 9 & 8\ 7 \\ 3 & - & \sharp & - \end{matrix}$$

e: ___ ___ ___ ___ ___ ___

e: i vii°⁶ i i⁶ iv V VI

9.89 Sometimes the resolution of one suspension becomes the preparation of another. This results in a "chain of suspensions."

Haydn, *Symphony No. 101* (*The Clock*)

Chains of suspensions are usually part of a harmonic and/or melodic sequence.* The brackets in the above example identify the sequence pattern.

(No response.)

_____
*Sequence is the repetition of musical pattern at a different pitch level.

S   S   S   S
PT   PT

PT

S
PT NT

PT   NT

9.90   Complete the alto and tenor voices and label all nonharmonic tones.

Bach, Chorale: *Heut' ist, o Mensch,*
ein Grosser Trauertag

8   -♭79 8 8-7 9 8   8 -♭6 5 6
4   3-   43-   4 4   3 3 3 3

B♭: V⁶——V   I

Note: This rather complicated phrase contains many nonharmonic tones (five suspensions, five passing tones and two neighboring tones). See how many you can identify properly.

9.91   One or more notes may appear between a suspension and its resolution. These are called ORNAMENTATIONS and most take the form of nonharmonic tones.

SINGLE TONE ORNAMENTATIONS

(1)   A   (2)   ET

(3)   App   (4)   chord
                               tone

The ornament in (1) consists of an anticipation of the resolution; ornaments in the form of the escape tone and the appoggiatura are shown in (2) and (3); example (4) shows that a chord tone may be in-

resolution   serted between a suspension and its _____

9.92   Ornamentations may consist of two or more tones.

In (1) the B is a lower neighboring tone to the anticipation (C); the E in example (2) is an upper neighboring tone; although rare, florid ornamentations such as in (3) are sometimes encountered (see the following frame).

Ornamentations introduce melodic activity between a suspension and its resolution and may in some cases delay the resolution; but no matter how it is ornamented, the resolution (in relation to the suspension) is by step. Do the majority of suspensions resolve

upward or downward? _____

downward

9.93   Ornamentations occur frequently when suspensions are woven into a complex contrapuntal fabric. Such a case is shown below where the florid ornamentation is part of the imitative procedure as is shown by the brackets.

Bach, *Well-Tempered Clavier*, Vol. 1, Fugue XXIV

Ornamentation is used to increase melodic activity and give variety to suspension figures. Suspensions are ornamented by inserting a note (or notes) between the preparation and the suspension.

(True/False) _____

False.
(Ornamentation occurs between the suspension and its resolution.)

9.94 Complete the alto and tenor voices and label each nonharmonic tone. In the case of suspensions indicate the preparation (P), suspension (S), and ornamentation (O).

Bach, Chorale: *Das alte Jahr vergangen ist*

This example shows that the bass (as well as other voices) may move as the suspension resolves. The above is a 9-8 type suspension; but due to the movement in the bass, the result is actually a 9-6 suspension.

9.95 There may also be a change of harmony as the suspension resolves. This is shown at the asterisk.

Bach, Chorale: *Christ lag in Todesbanden*

The suspension and its resolution do not always occur over the

bass   same _____note.

a: i   i   V⁶   i   VII⁶

III III⁶ VII i   V V   i

B♭: V⁶   I IV⁶ V   I

V ————— I

9.96   In the following example, complete the alto and tenor voices and label each nonharmonic tone. In the case of suspensions indicate each part of the figure. (Use the symbol P, S, R and O). Analyze.

Bach, Chorale: *Danket dem Herren, denn er ist sehr freundlich*

5 - 9 8 7 6   9 766-8721   4 3 2 #
2 -   5 ——
2 -

a: ___ ___ ___ ___ ___ ___

Note: This phrase contains six suspensions; label each carefully.

9.97   Continue as in the preceding frame.

Bach, Chorale: *Es spricht der Unweisen Mund*

6 5   5 - 8   8 7 2 1   5 4 - 5
       3 - 6   4 3 2 3
       3 3

B♭: ___ ___ ___ ___ ___

9.98   Suspensions cause dissonance to occur on the accented portions of the beat or measure; thus they contribute to a higher level of tension than unaccented nonharmonic tones. But since suspensions resolve by step, the result is a smooth, satisfying release from tension. The suspension is the most complex nonharmonic tone, so review carefully the principles which govern its use as stated on the next page:

1. The suspension occurs on a *strong* beat or portion of a beat.

2. The resolution usually occurs on the *weak* beat (or portion of a beat) immediately following the suspension.

3. The preparation is the same pitch as the suspension and is usually equal to or longer than the time value of the suspension.

4. The suspension resolves by step either upward or downward, but the majority resolve downward, (Suspensions which resolve upward are sometimes called *retardations*.)

5. The preparation is usually sustained into the suspension (often by the use of a tie), but the suspension may also be re-sounded. (some writers refer to such suspensions as *appoggiaturas*.)

6. Suspensions are classified according to the intervals which occur above the bass. The following types result: 4-3, 7-6, 9-8, 2-1, and 2-3.

7. Ornamentation consisting of one, two, or more tones may appear between the suspension and its resolution.

(No response.)

9.99   The example below shows nonharmonic tones which are called CHANGING TONES (symbol: CT):

Changing tones fall into a pattern of four notes, *the first and last of which are harmonic*. The second tone of the figure is approached by step and is left by a leap of a third in the opposite direction. The third tone (also nonharmonic) resolves by step to the final tone of the figure.

(No response.)

leap	9.100 In the changing tone figure the *first* nonharmonic tone is approached by step and the *second* by _____
step	9.101 The resolution of the *second* nonharmonic tone in the changing tone figure is by _____.
(3).	■ 9.102 Which example below shows changing tones? _____ (1) (2) (3)

9.103   You may wish to regard one of the nonharmonic tones of the changing tone figure as an ornamentation of a neighboring tone or passing tone.

    The second of the two changing tones in both (1) and (2) is an ornamentation of a neighboring tone; in (3) the first changing tone is an ornamentation of a passing tone. The ornamentation in (1) and (2) is in the form of an appoggiatura; the ornamentation in (3)

escape tone   is in the form of a(n) _____.

9.104 Circle and label all of the nonharmonic tones in the example below:

Berlioz, *Symphonie Fantastique*

9.105 When a tone is retained in one part while harmonies which are foreign to it are produced by other parts the effect is called PEDAL (symbol: Ped).*

Bach, *French Suite No. 1,* Allemande

The tone D in the lowest part is sustained while the upper parts produce independent harmonies. What relation does the pedal (D) have to the tonality of this example? It is the _____.

tonic

*This device is also called *pedal point,* or *organ point.*

9.106   The pedal device derives its name from the organist's technique of holding down a pedal while playing other harmonies above it. Pedals occur most frequently in the bass part. However, they may also occur in the upper or middle parts. The terms *inverted pedal* and *inner pedal* are sometimes used in such cases.

Bach, Chorale Prelude: *Vor deinen Thron tret' ich*

The pedal in the example above occurs in the highest

True.

voice. (True/False) _____

9.107   The pedal may be any scale degree, but it is usually either the tonic or dominant. Occasionally both the tonic and dominant are used simultaneously. The result is a double pedal.

Schumann, *Album for the Young,* Op. 68, No. 18

The pedal device gives a static quality in contrast to the harmonies with which it is associated. It tends to (strengthen/weaken)

strengthen

_____the tonality.

9.108   The pedal usually begins and ends as a harmonic tone. In this way its presence in the musical texture is "legitimized." Before proceeding to another tone, a pedal must be included once again as part of the harmony.

A nonharmonic tone which is approached and left by the same

True.

tone is called a pedal. (True/False) _____

9.109   The pedal is sometimes more than just a sustained tone. The example below shows a double pedal (A-A) which is part of a melodic figure. Note that the higher pedal is embellished by lower neighbors (G-sharps) to give added rhythmic interest.

Bach, *Well-Tempered Clavier*, Vol. 1 Prelude XX

Rhythmic and melodic figuration is used to counteract the tonally static quality of the pedal.

Which scale degree is stressed by the double pedal in the above

first

example? The _____ .

9.110   Since the pedal contributes greatly to tonal stability, accompanying harmony may be in sharp contrast to it. When double or triple pedals, or pedals with melodic significance are used, the effect is often of polyharmony or polytonality. Passages such as the one below are common in twentieth-century music.

Stravinsky, *Le Sacre du Printemps*

The triad sounded by the flutes is an example of a (single/

triple

double/triple) _____ pedal.

9.111   All of the nonharmonic tones presented thus far have been no more than a second away from either the preceding or succeeding tone. One nonharmonic tone, however, is both approached and left by leap. This type of nonharmonic tone is called a FREE TONE (symbol: FT).

Chopin, *Valse Brillante, Op. 34, No. 2*

leap	The free tone is the only nonharmonic tone which is approached and left by _____.
(3).	9.112 The free tone is the rarest of all nonharmonic tones so it will not be stressed here. In most cases it can be analyzed as part of a more complex sonority. The free tone in the preceding frame, for example, could be considered the eleventh of an expanded dominant sonority. Which example below shows a free tone? _____ (1) (2) (3) C: vii°6 I6 vii°6 I vii°6 I

Summary

Nonharmonic tones are extraneous to the harmony. Most nonharmonic tones appear in such a way that chords retain their integrity. In other words, the nonharmonic tone cannot be mistaken for a chord tone. Some tones, however, can be analyzed as being either harmonic or nonharmonic. For this reason, the chord first should be identified clearly. Thus, any tone that does not fall into the chord as *analyzed* must be a nonharmonic tone.

Later on in *Harmonic Materials and Tonal Music: Part II*, Chapter 3.0 it will be found that nonharmonic tones may also be chromatically altered to supply further tonal color and variety. These "altered" nonharmonic tones are used to bring attention to particular harmonies as well. The most frequent alterations found are the *raised fourth* and the *lowered seventh* scale degrees.

The rhythmic activity which nonharmonic tones give to each part contributes to the independence of the melodic lines. Greater smoothness is another result of good nonharmonic tone usage. Of still greater importance, however, is the introduction of dissonance to the musical texture. Although not all nonharmonic tones are dissonant, most are. Dissonant tones which immediately resolve into more consonant ones cause an ebb and flow of tensions, which help produce the effect of forward motion.

Nonharmonic tones provide the composer with the means of introducing dissonance into music to whatever degree desired. Nonharmonic dissonance, however, is fleeting; it is tightly controlled in accordance with established practice and is readily tolerated by the listener.

The various types of nonharmonic tones are summarized and illustrated in the chart that follows.

SUMMARY OF NONHARMONIC TONES

Name	Symbol	Example	Approach	Left	Direction of Resolution
Passing tone (unaccented or accented)	PT	PT ... PT	By step	By step	Same as approach
Neighboring tone (unaccented or accented)	NT	NT ... NT	By step	By step	Opposite to approach
Appoggiatura (unaccented or accented)	App	App ... App	By leap (The App. may be the initial tone)	By step	Usually opposite to approach
Escape tone	ET	ET ... ET	By step	By leap	Usually opposite to approach
Anticipation	A	A ... A	Usually by step	By the same tone	Same tone

SUMMARY OF NONHARMONIC TONES

Name	Symbol	Example	Approach	Left	Direction of Resolution
Suspension	S		By the same tone (tied or reiterated)	By step	Up or down
Changing tones	CT		By step or leap	By step or leap	Usually the same tone as the approach
Pedal	Ped		By the same tone	By the same tone	Same tone
Free tone	FT		By leap	By leap	Usually opposite to approach

Mastery Frames

9–1   Name the nonharmonic tone described in each case.

(1)   Approached by step and left by repetition.

(1)   Anticipation   (9.61–.65)

_____

(2)   Approached and left by step in the same direction.

(2)   Passing tone   (9.15–.33)

_____

(3)   Approached by step and left by leap.

(3)   Escape tone   (9.50–.55)

_____

(4)   Approached by leap and left by step.

(4)   Appoggiatura   (9.42–.49)

_____

(5)   Approached and left by step with a change in direction.

(5)   Neighboring tone   (9.34–.41)

_____

(6)   Approached by the same tone and left by step.

(6)   Suspension   (9.69–.98)

_____

9–2   Identify the three parts of the suspension figure shown below.

(1)   Preparation   (1) _____

(2)   Suspension   (2) _____

(3)   Resolution   (3) _____

(9.70–.73)

2–3. (9.81)	9–3 Which of the suspension types (4-3, 7-6, 9-8, or 2-3) would be found in the bass voice? _____
(1) Changing tones (9.99–.104) (2) Free tone (9.111–.112) (3) Retardation (9.75)	9–4 Name the nonharmonic tones at the asterisks. (1) _____ (2) _____ (3) _____ d: i ——————— C: I V⁶ G: V I⁶ I
pedal (9.100–.110)	9–5 A tone that is retained in one part (usually the bass) while harmonies which are foreign to it are produced by other parts is called a _____.

Supplementary Assignments

ASSIGNMENTS 9–1   Name _____

1. Circle all nonharmonic tones and label with abbreviations (PT, NT, etc.).

2. Write nonharmonic tones as directed. (*Notes may be added to the soprano or bass parts. Also, use accidentals when needed to produce the chord quality indicated by the Roman numerals. Irregular doubling may be needed to facilitate creation of nonharmonic tones.*)

3. Write the three upper voices to fulfill the requirements.

ASSIGNMENTS 9–2   Name

1. Rewrite the soprano part to show three different ornamentations of the suspension.

2. Write the alto and tenor voices according to the figured bass symbols. Label all nonharmonic tones and provide the Roman numeal analysis.

3. Supply four-voice harmonizations for the melodies below which include the nonharmonic tones indicated. Also provide the Roman numeral analysis.

4. Compose a short work for the piano (or other media, at the discretion of your instructor). Be guided by the items below.

   (1) Length: 4-8 phrases
   (2) Homophonic texture
   (3) Meter and key of your choice
   (4) Piano styles 2-18 are recomended
   (5) Make liberal use of nonharmonic tones in the melody
   (6) Identify all nonharmonic tones
   (7) Do a harmonic analysis
   (8) Use complete notation

Appendix A
Chord Symbols

Since early in the nineteenth century, symbols have been used to show the harmonic function of chords. These symbols consist of Roman and Arabic numerals as well as letters, accidentals, and figures such as the circle and plus sign. Chord symbols provide a vocabulary for verbal and written reference, and serve as a quick means of identifying not only a chord's relation to the tonal center, but also its quality and structure.

Musical analysis may take many forms, ranging from mere descriptive observation to complex interpretations made with reference to some explanatory system. Symbolism varies with the degree of exactness required by the analysis. The symbols used in this book are a compromise between simplicity and exactness; they may easily be adapted to serve the purpose of a particular type of analysis. Inversions, for example, generally are shown as part of the chord symbol; but, if the purpose of analysis is served merely by showing how chords function in a progression, symbols may be simplified by representing chords in root position only. Chord symbols are not precise enough to permit music to be reconstructed from them alone. They do, however, indicate the specific quality of diatonic triads and seventh chords (either directly or by inference) and usually show inversions. Thus the basic harmonic structure may readily be traced. In the case of certain altered chords, undue complexity is avoided at the expense of precision. To be completely consistent, logical and devoid of ambiguity, chord symbols would be so complex that many no longer would serve as convenient references to harmonic entities.

As in many areas of music theory, there is a lack of standardization regarding chord symbols. Whenever possible, the most widely accepted practices have been observed. The following information summarizes the symbols used in this book.

DIATONIC TRIADS

Roman numerals are used to identify triads and are directly related to scale degrees. Further, the quality of triads is shown by the form of the symbols (capital letters = major, small letters = minor, small letters with circle = diminished, and capital letters with plus sign = augmented.)

315

First and second inversions of triads are shown by adding the figured bass symbols 6 or $\frac{6}{4}$ to the Roman numerals.

Notice that the figures are placed at the upper right-hand corner of the Roman numerals. When more than one number is involved, the largest appears at the top and the remainder are placed in descending order.

SYMBOLS FOR CHORDS NOT PRESENTED IN THIS BOOK

Some of the examples in this book include chords which are not treated fully until HMTM Part II. In no case does comprehension of the material depend upon an understanding of these chords.

DIATONIC SEVENTH CHORDS

The figure 7 added to the Roman numeral indicates a seventh chord in root position. In a major key the form of the Roman numeral is the same as for the corresponding triad.

The symbols used in harmonic minor are shown below:

Notice that in the diminished minor, or so-called "half-diminished" seventh chord (ii$^{\phi 7}$, vii$^{\phi 7}$), the circle which denotes the diminished triad is replaced by a circle with a slash. For the fully diminished, or so-called "diminished" seventh chord (vii$^{\circ 7}$), the circle which denotes the diminished triad is an indicator that the seventh is diminished as well. All half or fully diminished seventh chords are shown in these ways regardless of their use. This attempts to keep the nomenclature in comformity with that used by many writers and instructors. As somewhat traditional symbols, the circle and circle with slash are appropriate in reflecting the theoretical practices currently in use.

Inversions of seventh chords are shown by figured bass symbols.

THE DOMINANT NINTH CHORD

The symbol V^9 is used to represent a dominant chord consisting of four superimposed thirds.

THE MEDIANT MAJOR TRIAD IN MINOR KEYS

The mediant generated by the descending form of the melodic minor scale is a major triad. The chord symbol is an upper-case Roman numeral. For example:

Creative writing is possibly the best way to demonstrate command of the concepts and materials presented in this text. In original compositions students may apply the knowledge gained in terms of their own creativity. It is desirable that a variety of media (piano, voice, small ensembles, etc.) be used, but because of its availability, the piano is the most practical. The brief exposition of piano styles presented here provides a guide for those who have had litttle experience with keyboard techniques.* Effective writing is possible — even by non-pianists — if typical styles are utilized. The material which follows — used in conjunction with the suggested supplementary assignments — facilitates the creative work which helps develop a heightened sensitivity to the rhetoric of harmonic music.

There are three textures into which all music falls: *monophonic* (a single melodic line), *homophonic* (a melody with accompaniment); and *polyphonic* (several voices approximately equal in melodic interest). Of these, homophonic texture is the most practical for music in which the harmonic element is stressed. Thus we shall concentrate on various homophonic piano styles.

■ All of the following examples (①- ㉛) are reproduced on the cassette or compact disc.

I. FIGURATED BLOCK CHORDS. In the example below, the melody is provided a simple accompaniment in block chords.

Mozart: *Sonata*, K 545 (altered)

*Some of the examples contain harmonic materials presented in HMTM Part II.

Block chords are easy to play because the left hand does not move over the keyboard. Care should be taken that principles of doubling and voice leading are applied. Active tones (the leading tone and chord sevenths) should not be doubled, and should be resolved properly. Notice in measure two, for example, that the leading tone (B) is omitted from the left hand and also that the chord seventh (F) is resolved down by step to E.

Figuration patterns give rhythmic interest to block chords.

Mozart: *Sonata*, K 545

The way that the three notes of the block chords are transcribed into the figuration pattern is clear.

This technique of providing rhythmic animation for block chords is called "Alberti bass," after the Venetian composer Dominico Alberti (1710-1740?), who used such patterns extensively, perhaps even to excess.

Styles 3-12 show some of the many figurations which may be devised. The meter, as well as the degree of animation desired, affects the choice of pattern.

II. JUMP BASS (AFTER-BEAT PATTERNS). In these styles the left hand jumps from bass notes to block chords. The best sonority results when the block chords are set in the vicinity of middle C.

Schubert: *Waltz in A minor*

As in figured block chords, care must be taken that principles of part writing are observed. In the above example there are four voices in the left hand. Notice how each of these traces a smooth line, and also the way active tones resolve properly.

Of course the relation of the accompanying voices to the melody must also be considered. *Undesirable doubling and incorrect parallel motion must be avoided.*

Jump bass patterns are exploited mostly in waltzes and mazurkas, but are also useful in duple or quadruple meter for march-like effects. Some typical patterns are shown in styles 14-18.

III. APPEGGIATION   The successive sounding of chord tones over a more or less extended range is called arpeggiation. Compared with previously presented styles, arpeggiation generally produces more sonorous effects. This is due to the vibration of more strings. Rhythmic animation and richer texture also result from arpeggiation.

There is scarcely any limit to the arpeggiation patterns which can be devised. The examples which follow demonstrate a few typical patterns; these may suggest others which satisfy specific expressive needs as they arise.

In style 19, arpeggiation is used exclusively throughout the entire composition. The effect is of figurated harmonies.

Schumann: *Album für die Jugend* ("Kleine Studie")

The example below shows fairly simple left hand arpeggiation, which supports a melody in the right hand.

Chopin: *Nocturne,* Posthumous

The arpeggiation in the next example is more extended in range.

Leybach: *Nocturne*, Op. 52

Style 22 has an arpeggiation pattern in the left hand while the right hand not only plays the melody but also fills in the harmony for additional sonority.

Brahms: *Intermezzo,* Op. 119, No. 2

Arpeggiation takes a different form in the next example. The treble and bass move mostly in parallel tenths, while the middle voice completes the harmony, and fills in the eighth note rhythm.

Mendelssohn, *Lieder ohne Worte*, Op. 85, No. 2

In style 24 the arpeggiation is in the tenor register, divided between the right and left hand.

Schumann: *Kinderscenen* ("Von Fremden Ländern und Menschen")

In the next example the arpeggiation is in descending motion, divided between the two hands.

Burgmüller: *Lullaby*

IV. HYMN STYLE For serious, dignified or stately effects, melodies may be accompanied in a fashion
similar to vocal settings of hymns. In this style chords change for almost every melody note. The resulting
rapid harmonic rhythm makes figuration impractical. The number of voices may be consistent, or fluctuate
to produce the desired sonorities.
   Close style: The example below shows octave doubling of the bass, with the remaining voices in the right
hand.

Schumann: *Album für die Jugend* ("Nordisches Lied"), Op. 26

   Open style: In this case the voices are divided equally between the two hands and open structure
predominates. Only once is the four-part texture enriched by the addition of a fifth tone.

Chopin: *Mazurka*, Op. 68, No. 3

V. RIGHT-HAND PATTERNS.

Of the several typical ways to treat the right hand, the single line melody is the simplest. This style has been amply demonstrated in previous examples (see styles 2, 13, 20, and 21). A few others are shown in the remaining examples.

Added alto in thirds and sixths:

Mozart: *Sonata*, K 333

Filled in chords:

Schubert: *Waltz in B-flat Major*

Melody in octaves: Increased sonority and promenince for the melodic line can be supplied by octave doubling.

Beethoven: *Sonata*, Op. 10, No. 1

Melody with after beats: This technique is used when fuller sonorities are desired. Such patterns also produce a more intricate rhythmic texture.

Mendelssohn: *Lieder ohne Worte*, Op. 102, No. 1

Polyphonic texture has not been touched on here, but even casual use of imitation between melodic and accompaniment elements is effective. In addition, placement of the melody in the tenor or bass registers with the accompaniment above, provides variety. Above all, avoid using only a limited range. The compass of the piano is more than seven octaves, and effective writing requires that the hands range rather widely over the keyboard. In this way the color contrasts of the various registers are exploited.

A

Accessory Tone *See* Nonharmonic tone.

Accidental A sign that affects the pitch of a note.

Acoustics The science that deals with sound.

Active tone A tone that has a strong tendency to resolve in a specific direction, *e.g.*, the leading tone.

Altered chord A chord that contains one or more tones which are foreign to the prevailing tonality. Most altered chords fall into four classes: secondary dominants, borrowed chords, chromatic mediants, and augmented sixth chords.

Altered dominants Dominant triads or seventh chords with heightened activity due to chromatic alteration of the fifth.

Altered nonharmonic tone A nonharmonic tone that is inflected so as to be foreign to the prevailing tonality.

Altered tone A tone that is not included in the prevailing tonality.

Alto A low female voice. The next-to-the-highest voice of the four-part chorus.

Amen cadence *See* Plagal cadence.

Anticipation A nonharmonic tone that is approached by step and left by repetition.

Appoggiatura A nonharmonic tone that is approached by leap and left by step, usually with a change of direction.

Appoggiatura chord A chord that is used in a nonharmonic capacity similar to the appoggiatura.

Arpeggiation Sounding the tones of a chord in succession, rather than simultaneously.

Arpeggio six-four chord A second inversion chord formed by arpeggiated movement in the lowest voice.

Atonality The absence of a tonal center.

Augmented fourth An interval that is a half step larger than a perfect fourth.

Augmented major seventh chord A seventh chord consisting of an augmented triad plus a major seventh.

Augmented second An interval that is a half step larger than a major second.

Augmented six-five chord *See* German sixth chord.

Augmented six-four-three chord *See* French sixth chord.

Augmented six-three chord *See* Italian sixth chord.

Augmented sixth An interval that is a half step larger than a major sixth.

Augmented sixth chords A group of chords, all of which contain the interval of an augmented sixth (or diminished third). *See* French sixth chord, German sixth chord, and Italian sixth chord.

Augmented triad A chord consisting of two major thirds.

Authentic cadence A closing harmonic progression consisting of the dominant chord (sometimes the leading tone) followed by the tonic chord.

Auxilliary six-four chord *See* Pedal six-four chord.

Auxilliary tone *See* Neighboring tone.

B

Baroque era The musical period from 1600 to 1750 characterized by elaborate ornamentation, strict forms, and the establishment of functional harmonic tonality.

Bass A low male voice. Lowest voice of the four-part chorus.

Bass staff The staff modified by the bass clef sign, which desgnates F below middle C as occurring on the fourth line.

Borrowed chord A diatonic chord in one mode (major or minor), which appears as an altered chord in the opposite parallel mode. Most borrowed chords appear in major, borrowed from the parallel minor key.

Bytone *See* Nonharmonic tone.

C

Cadence A melodic-harmonic formula that brings a phrase to a more or less definite close.

Cadential six-four chord A second inversion chord that is part of a cadence formula – most frequently, the tonic chord in second inversion followed by the dominant.

Chain of suspensions Several suspensions in succession in which the resolution of one suspension becomes the preparation for the following.

Change of mode A change from major to minor (or the reverse) with the same tonal center retained.

Changing tone *See* Neighboring tone.

Changing tones The middle two notes of a four-note figure, of which the first and fourth are chord tones, and the second and third are nonharmonic tones.

Chord A combination of several tones, usually three or more, sounded simultaneously.

Chord changes Changes of harmony.

Chord function Chords function differently depending upon the relation of their root to the tonal center. The tonic chord, for example, is relatively static, whereas the dominant chord is active.

Chord of repose The tonic triad.

Chord quality Chords differ in quality according to their intervallic structure. Diatonic triads, for example, may be major, minor, diminished, or augmented.

Chord seventh The chord member that is a seventh above the root.

Chord spacing The placement of the various chord members in part writing. *See* Close structure; Open structure.

Chord symbol A figure composed of a Roman numeral and sometimes various figured bass symbols. Chord symbols identify the root of the chord in relation to the key center, as well as the quality.

Chord tone One of the tones that constitute a chord.

Chromatic 1) Melodic movement by half steps. 2) Music that incorporates many tones and chords foreign to the prevailing tonality.

Chromatic harmony Harmony that features many altered chords and frequent modulations to foreign keys.

Chromatic mediants Chords whose roots are related by the interval of a third and that contain one or more tones foreign to a single diatonic scale.

Chromatic modulation 1) Modulation in which not all voices move diatonically. 2) Modulation to a foreign key. 3) Modulation in which the common chord is an altered chord in one or both of the keys involved.

Chromatic movement Half-step movement that involves only one basic note.

Chromatic scale A scale consisting entirely of half steps.

Chromatic third relation *See* Chromatic mediants.

Chromatic third-relation harmony *See* Chromatic mediants.

Classical era The musical period from about 1750 to 1800, characterized by simplicity and order.

Closely related keys Keys whose signatures differ by not more than one sharp or flat.

Close structure The spacing of voices so that no vacant chord members occur between the three upper voices.

Color harmony *See* Nonfunctional harmony.

Common chord A chord that functions in two or more keys.

Common chord modulation A modulation that involves a common chord.

Common tone A tone that occurs in two or more chords.

Consecutive perfect intervals Perfect unisons, fourths, fifths, or octaves that occur in succession between the same two voices.

Contrary motion Two voices that move in opposite directions.

Crossed voices The abnormal vertical distribution of voices in a chord, *e.g.*, the alto placed above the soprano.

Cross relation *See* False relation.

D

Damper pedal The right-hand pedal of the piano, which, when depressed, allows the strings to continue vibrating.

Deceptive cadence A nonfinal cadence consisting of the dominant chord followed by the submediant chord.

Deceptive resolution An unexpected resolution of a chord. Typically, the resolution of the dominant chord to the submediant, rather than to the expected tonic.

Development section In sonata form, the section following the exposition. Previously stated themes undergo various types of variation, and there is usually frequent modulation.

Diatonic Literally "by step"— having to do with scale tones; tonal material derived from a scale.

Diatonic modulation A modulation that involves diatonic melodic movement, and in which the common chord is a diatonic chord in both keys.

Diatonic scale A scale limited to the half and whole steps.

Diatonic seventh chords Seventh chords that are limited to tones of a diatonic scale.

Diatonic triad A triad consisting of tones included in a scale.

Diminished fifth An interval that is a half step smaller than a perfect fifth.

Diminished-minor seventh chord A seventh chord consisting of a diminished triad plus a minor seventh.

Diminished seventh chord A seventh chord consisting of a diminished triad plus a diminished seventh.

Diminished third An interval that is a half step smaller than a minor third.

Diminished triad A chord consisting of two minor thirds.

Dissonance Auditory tension produced by two or more tones when sounding intervals of the major or minor second, major or minor seventh, or tritone.

Dissonant elements A chord member or nonharmonic tone that creates a dissonance, *e.g.*, the chord seventh.

Distant keys *See* Foreign keys.

Dominant The fifth degree of the scale, or the chord built thereupon.

Dominant eleventh chord A chord of six tones built in thirds on the fifth scale degree.

Dominant function A chord that relates to the following chord as a dominant or leading tone triad, seventh, ninth, etc.

Dominant ninth chord A chord of five tones built in thirds on the fifth scale degree.

Dominant relation The relation between a dominant chord and its tonic.

Dominant seventh chord A chord of four tones built in thirds on the fifth scale degree, a major-minor seventh chord.

Dominant seventh chord with lowered fifth Equivalent to the French sixth chord built on the lowered second scale degree.

Dominant thirteenth chord A chord of seven tones built in thirds on the fifth scale degree.

Double flat A sign that causes a basic note to be lowered in pitch a whole step.

Double pedal Two tones (usually tonic and dominant) used simultaneously as a pedal.

Double sharp A sign that causes a basic note to be raised in pitch a whole step.

Doubled tones The same chord member sung by two or more voices.

Doubling The assignment of the same chord member to two or more voices. This is necessary when a triad is set for four or more voices.

Doubly augmented six-four-three chord A German sixth chord with the perfect fifth above the sounding root spelled enharmonically as a doubly augmented fourth.

Downward stem A stem that extends downward from a notehead. When the grand staff is used for the four-voice chorus, alto and bass stems go downward.

Dyad A two-note chord.

Dynamics The aspect of music concerning varying degrees of loudness and softness.

Dynamic indications Signs that indicate varying degrees of loudness (amplitude).

E

Echappée *See* Escape tone.

Elements of Music The basic properties of music, which include rhythm, melody, timbre, texture, and harmony.

Eleventh chord A chord of six tones built in thirds.

Embellishing harmony The chords that are not vital to the stability of the phrase, in contrast to structural harmony.

Embellishing six-four chord *See* Pedal six-four chord.

Enharmonic change Alternate notation of the same pitch, *e.g.*, C-sharp changed to D-flat.

Enharmonic modulation Modulation in which there is an enharmonic change of one or more notes.

Enharmonic spelling A single pitch spelled differently, *e.g.* G-sharp/A-flat.

Equal temperament Tuning of the tones contained within an octave so that all half steps are of equal size.

Escape tone A nonharmonic tone that is approached by step and left by leap, usually with a change of direction.

Essential chord A chord that serves a structural function; often one of the three primary triads (tonic, subdominant, or dominant).

Essential dissonance Dissonance that is part of the harmony.

Expanded tertian sonorities Chords constructed by adding thirds above the triad (seventh, ninth, eleventh, and thirteenth chords).

F

False relation Chromaticism that occurs between two different voices.

Fifteenth The interval of a double octave.

Figured bass A shorthand notation widely used during the Baroque era. *See* Figured bass symbols.

Figured bass symbols Various signs, including numerals and accidentals, placed beneath the bass to indicate chords and melodic motion in the upper voices. Figured bass symbols basically show the intervals that occur above the lowest voice.

Final cadences The cadences that produce a sufficient sense of closure to conclude principal sections of the music. The two final cadences are the authentic and plagal.

First inversion A chord that employs the third in the lowest voice.

Flat A sign that causes a basic note to be lowered in pitch a half step.

Foreign keys Keys whose signatures differ by more than one sharp or flat.

Foreign tone *See* Nonharmonic tone.

Four-part texture Music set in four parts. *See* Four-voice chorus.

Four-part writing Music set in four parts.

Four-voice chorus A chorus consisting of soprano, alto, tenor, and bass.

Free tone A nonharmonic tone that is approached and left by leap.

French sixth chord An augmented sixth chord consisting of a major third, augmented fourth, and augmented sixth above a given note. The French sixth chord is sometimes called an augmented six-four-three chord.

Functional harmony The employment of chords and root progressions that serve to establish a tonality.

G

German sixth chord An augmented sixth chord consisting of a major third, perfect fifth, and augmented sixth above a given note. The German sixth chord is sometimes called an augmented six-five chord.

Grand staff Two staves joined together, usually with the treble clef sign on the upper and the bass clef sign on the lower.

Gregorian chant The monodic liturgical music of the Roman Catholic Church.

H

Half cadence A nonfinal cadence, usually terminating with the dominant chord.

Half step The smallest interval of the tempered scale, equivalent to a minor second.

Harmonic action The effect of chords moving from one to another.

Harmonic analysis The process of examining critically the harmonic element of music. The identification of tonalities and the labeling of chords are basic types of harmonic analysis.

Harmonic cadence Closure produced by harmonic action. The strong dominant-tonic progression, for example, contributes to the positive effect of the authentic cadence irrespective of the rhythmic and melodic elements.

Harmonic function The movement of chords to one another defines tonal space and delineates form. Harmonic function basically is either "structural" or "embellishing."

Harmonic interval The interval produced by two tones sounding simultaneously.

Harmonic minor scale A scale that consists of the following half- and whole-step pattern: W H W W H W+ H H.

Harmonic phrase A succession of chords that constitutes a phrase.

Harmonic progression The movement from one chord to another.

Harmonic rhythm The rhythm defined by chord changes.

Harmonic sequence The successive repetition of a harmonic pattern at a different pitch.

Harmonic tension Tension created by the use of relatively dissonant chords.

Harmonic tonality The definition of a tonal center by means of chords relating in various ways to the tonic.

Harmonic tone A tone that is included as part of a chord.

Harmonization The technique of selecting chords to accompany a melody.

Harmony The element of music concerning chords and their relation to one another.

Horizontal aspect of harmony Successions of chords.

I

Imperfect cadence An authentic or plagal cadence that lacks a complete sense of finality. *See* perfect cadence.

Impressionist music Music that utilizes techniques developed by impressionist composers, particularly Debussy and Ravel. Features of this music include liberal use of expanded tertian sonorities, unresolved dissonance, parallelism, the whole tone and pentatonic scales, and flexible rhythms.

Inactive tones Tones of the tonic triad are relatively inactive unless part of a dissonant sonority.

Inner pedal An alternate term for a pedal that occurs in an inner voice. *See* Pedal.

Interval The difference in pitch between two tones.

Inversion 1) Altering an interval so that the higher note be comes the lower. This is usually done by moving the upper note an octave lower, or vice versa. 2) Placing a chord member other than the root in the bass.

Inverted pedal An alternate term for a pedal that occurs in an upper voice. *See* Pedal.

Irregular doubling The exigencies of part writing sometimes make it necessary to employ an alternate doubling to avoid a more serious weakness.

Italian sixth chord An augmented sixth chord consisting of a major third and augmented sixth above a given note. The Italian sixth chord is sometimes called an augmented six-three chord.

Iteration Emphasis by repetition, immediate or delayed.

K

Key The tonality of a composition or segment thereof.

Key center The tonal center; the first degree of the scale upon which the music is based.

Key signature A group of sharps or flats that produce the desired half- and whole-step pattern of a given scale.

Keynote *See* tonal center.

L

Leading tone The seventh scale degree (a half step below the tonic), or the chord built thereupon.

Leading tone relation A chord that relates to the following chord as a leading tone triad, seventh chord, etc.

Leading tone seventh chord A chord of four tones built in thirds on the seventh scale degree (a half step below the tonic).

M

Major key The tonality formed by a major scale.

Major-minor-major ninth chord A ninth chord consisting of a major triad, a minor seventh, and major ninth; a dominant ninth chord in a major key

Major-minor seventh chord A seventh chord consisting of a major triad plus a minor seventh; the dominant seventh chord.

Major ninth chord Equivalent to a dominant ninth chord in a major key.

Major scale A scale that consists of the following half- and whole-step pattern: W W H W W W H.

Major seventh chord A seventh chord consisting of a major triad plus a major seventh.

Major triad A chord consisting of a major third and a superimposed minor third.

Mediant The third scale degree, or the chord built thereupon.

Mediant relationship Chords whose roots are the interval of a third apart are in a mediant relationship with one another.

Mediant seventh chord A seventh chord built on the third scale degree.

Melodic activity Interest created by the melodic element of music.

Melodic contour The shape defined by the rising and falling pitches of a melody.

Melodic function Performance of a linear, rather than a harmonic role.

Melodic line *See* Melodic contour.

Melodic minor scale A scale that consists of two forms:
Ascending: W H W W W W H
Descending: W W H W W H W

Melodic phrase A phrase etched by the melodic contour.

Melodic sequence The successive repetition of a melodic unit at a different pitch.

Melody A musical line produced by a series of single tones.

Minor-major seventh chord A seventh chord consisting of a minor triad plus a major seventh.

Minor ninth chord Equivalent to a dominant ninth chord in a minor key.

Minor seventh chord A seventh chord consisting of a minor triad plus a minor seventh.

Minor triad A chord consisting of a minor third and a superimposed major third.

Modal mixture The exchange of diatonic chords between parallel major and minor keys.

Modulating sequence A melodic and/or harmonic pattern stated successively at different pitch levels and in different keys.

Modulation The act of establishing a new tonal center.

N

Natural minor scale A minor scale that uses the same tones as its relative major scale. It consists of the following half- and whole-step pattern: W H W W H W W.

Neapolitan sixth chord A major triad built on the lowered second scale degree, usually in the first inversion.

Neighboring tone A nonharmonic tone that is approached and left by step with a change of direction. Neighboring tones usually occur on an unaccented portion of the beat and may be either a step above or below the harmonic tone.

New key The tonal destination of a modulation.

Ninth chord A chord of five tones built in thirds.

Nonchord tone *See* Nonharmonic tone.

Nondominant seventh chord Any seventh chord other than the dominant seventh.

Nonfinal cadences Cadences that are incapable of bringing a composition to a close. The two nonfinal cadences are the half and the deceptive.

Nonfunctional Harmony that performs an embellishing, rather than a tonality-defining role.

Nonharmonic tone A tone that is extraneous to the harmony.

Normal resolution The usual, predictable movement of an active tone or chord.

Notehead The part of a note that indicates the pitch.

O

Oblique motion Movement of two voices, one of which remains stationery while the other moves either upward or downward.

Octave An interval in which the frequency of the higher note is double that of the lower.

Old key The original tonality of a modulation.

Open structure The spacing of voices so that there is a vacant chord member between the tenor and alto, and between the alto and soprano.

Opening progression Harmonic movement away from the tonic at the beginning of the phrase.

Organ point *See* Pedal.

Ornamentation One or more notes appearing between a suspension and its resolution.

P

Pandiatonicism The use of the tone of a diatonic scale without observing their usual functional idiosyncrasies.

Parallel keys Two keys (major and minor) that employ the same tonic.

Parallel fifths Movement in fifths between the same two voices. If both fifths are perfect, the individuality of the voices is diminished. Such movement is generally avoided.

Parallel motion Two or more voices moving by the same intervals in the same direction.

Parallel perfect fifths Movement in perfect fifths between the same two voices. Such movement is generally avoided.

Part writing The technique of writing chords and leading voices from one to another.

Passing chord A chord that performs a nonharmonic function similar to a passing tone.

Passing six-four chord A second-inversion chord that usually occurs between a triad in first inversion and the same triad in root position. Typical is the following: tonic in first inversion — dominant in second inversion — tonic in root position.

Passing tone A nonharmonic tone that is approached and left by step in the same direction. It may occur either ascending or descending, and may be either accented or unaccented.

Passive resolution The retention of an active tone, *e.g.*, the chord seventh, in the same voice in the following chord.

Pedal A nonharmonic tone that is sustained (usually in the bass), against which other voices produce harmonies that are foreign to it.

Pedal point *See* Pedal.

Pedal six-four chord A second-inversion chord that

occurs over the same (or repeated) bass note, *e.g.*, the subdominant six-four preceded and followed by the tonic in root position.

Perfect cadence An authentic or plagal cadence that meets the following conditions:
1. Both the final and penultimate chords must be in root position.
2. The final (tonic) chord must have the keynote in the highest voice.

Phrase A basic unit in the formal organization of music, usually four measures in length, used especially during the classical period.

Phrase modulation A modulation that occurs at the beginning of a new phrase.

Phrase structure The underlying harmonies stripped of embellishing chords. Most phrases fall into one of three types:
1. A single chord followed by a cadence.
2. Harmonic embellishment by a single chord followed by a cadence.
3. A cadence formula (or basic harmonic progression) spread over the entire phrase.

Phrygian cadence In traditional harmony, a type of half cadence. The subdominant in first inversion moving to the dominant (in a minor key) is a typical example.

Picardy third The raised third in the tonic chord of a minor key. This effect is usually reserved for the final chord, to provide a more emphatic conclusion.

Pitch The "highness" or "lowness" of sound.

Pivot chord *See* Common chord.

Pivot tone A single tone that is common to two keys and serves as a link from one to the other.

Pivot tone modulation Modulation by means of a tone that is common to two keys.

Plagal cadence A closing harmonic progression consisting of the subdominant chord followed by the tonic chord.

Polychord Two or more chords sounding simultaneously.

Polyharmony Two or more chords that occur simultaneously.

Polytonality The simultaneous occurrence of two or more tonalities.

Preparation The initial note of the suspension figure. *See* Suspension.

Primary triads The tonic, subdominant, and dominant triads.

Progression 1) The movement from one chord to another. 2) More specifically, harmonic movement that creates a sense of forward motion. Root movements down in fifths, up in seconds, and down in thirds generally produce strong effects. *See also* Retrogression.

Pure minor scale See Natural scale.

R

Range The normal compass of a given voice or instrument.

Relative keys Major and minor keys that have the same signature, but different tonics.

Remote keys *See* Foreign keys.

Resolution 1) The movement from one chord to another; the term often denotes movement from an active chord to a less active one. 2) The final note of the suspension figure. *See also* Suspension.

Retardation Another term meaning an upward suspension. *See also* Suspension.

Retrogression A relatively weak harmonic movement.

See also Progression.

Returning note *See* Neighboring tone.

Rhythm The temporal aspect of music. Involved is the division of time into beats, accent patterns of meter, and rhythmic figures.

Roman numerals Symbols used to identify chords built on the various degrees of the scale.

Roman numeral analysis The use of Roman numerals and other figures associated with chord symbols to indicate the quality of chords and their position in relation to the key center.

Romantic era The musical period from about 1800 to 1900 characterized by emphasis on emotional qualities, freedom of form, increased use of chromaticism, and expanded tonality.

Root The note on which a chord is built.

Root movement The intervallic relationship of the root of a chord to the root of an adjoining chord.

Root position The arrangement of a chord so that the root is in the lowest voice.

S

Scale A stepwise arrangement (ascending or descending) of the tones contained in an octave.

Scale degrees The tones contained in a scale.

Secondary dominant An altered chord that functions as dominant (a leading tone) to a diatonic triad other than the tonic.

Secondary seventh chord *See* Nondominant seventh chords.

Secondary triads Triads that are built on the second, third, sixth, and seventh scale degrees.

Second inversion The arrangement of a triad so that the fifth is in the lowest voice

Sequence The successive statement or repetition of a melodic and/or harmonic unit at a different pitch level.

Sequence modulation Modulation caused by sequence units that move successively through different keys.

Sequential pattern A melodic and/or harmonic unit that is repeated successively at a different pitch.

Seventh 1) An interval encompassing seven basic notes. 2) The highest note of a seventh chord when in root position.

Seventh chord A chord consisting of four tones built in thirds.

Sharp A sign that causes a basic note to be raised a half step.

Signature *See* Key signature.

Similar motion Two voices that move in the same direction, but not by the same interval.

Six-four chord *See* Second inversion.

Slash (/) A sign that is used in connection with figured bass symbols. When drawn through a number, the note represented by the number is raised a half step.

Sonata form A form consisting of three principal sections: exposition, development, and recapitulation. Sometimes called "first movement" form because of its use in most opening movements of the classical symphony, sonata, and concerto.

Sonority The aural effect of a tone or group of tones.

Soprano A high female voice. The highest voice of the four-voice chorus.

Sounding root The chord member of the Italian and German sixth chords that has the aural effect of the root, as opposed to the "written" root. *See* Written root.

Spacing The placement of the various chord members in part writing. *See also* Chord spacing.

Staff The five parallel horizontal lines and intervening spaces upon which musical symbols are place.

Stationary six-four chord *See* Pedal six-four chord.

Stem The vertical line attached to a notehead.

Stepwise motion Melodic movement to adjacent scale degrees.

Strong beat A beat that has relatively strong metric stress, *e.g.*, the first beat of the measure.

Sructural harmony Harmony that appears at strategic formal points and serves to establish the tonal organization.

Structural points Locations that have special formal significance, *e.g.*, the beginning and end of the phrase.

Structural tones The first, fourth, and fifth tones of the scale are the roots of the three primary triads: tonic, subdominant, and dominant.

Structure of tonality The tonal pattern created by the three principal triads: the tonic, the dominant (a perfect fifth above), and the subdominant (a perfect fifth below).

Subdominant The fourth scale degree, or the chord built thereupon.

Subdominant seventh chord A seventh chord built on the fourth scale degree.

Submediant The sixth scale degree, or the chord built thereupon.

Submediant seventh chord A seventh chord built on the sixth scale degree.

Submediant seventh chord with raised root and third A diminished seventh chord built on the raised sixth scale degree in major. Resolution is usually to the dominant triad or seventh chord in first inversion.

Subtonic The tone a whole step below the tonic, or the chord built thereupon.

Supertonic The second scale degree, or the chord built thereupon.

Supertonic seventh chord A seventh chord built on the second scale degree.

Supertonic seventh chord with raised root and third A diminished seventh chord built on the raised second scale degree in major. Resolution is usually to the tonic chord in first inversion.

Suspended tonality The effect produced by a series of nonfunctional chords or rapid modulations.

Suspension A nonharmonic tone that is approached by the same note (usually tied) and left by step (usually downward).

Symmetrical chords Chords that incorporate some form of symmetry, *e.g.*, the augmented triad and the diminished seventh chords that divide the octave into equal intervals.

Symmetrical relationship Tones, chords, or rhythms that bear some kind of equal relationship to one another, *e.g.*, a passage of chords in which roots are related consistently by the interval of the third.

T

Tenor A high male voice. The next-to-the-lowest voice of the four-voice chorus.

Tension *See* Harmonic tension.

Texture The structure of sound created by tones sounding together.

Third inversion A chord that employs the seventh in the lowest voice.

Third relation Tones or chords related by the interval of the third.

Thirteenth chord A chord of seven tones built in thirds.

Timbre The quality of sound determined by the number and relative intensity of its overtones.

Tonal center The first degree of the scale: the tonic.

Tonal harmony Harmony based on diatonic scales that demonstrates loyalty toward the tonic.

Tonal music Music that adheres to a central tone, the tonic.

Tonal spectrum The array of tones utilized in a given passage or composition.

Tonal system *See* Tonality.

Tonal vocabulary The tonal resources available within a particular style.

Tonality The organization of the tones and chords of a key with reference to the tonic.

Tone cluster A relatively dissonant chord produced by sounding several tones close together.

Tonic The first degree of the scale, or the chord built thereupon.

Tonic-dominant axis The tonality-defining relationship governed by the tonic and dominant chords, whose roots are a perfect fifth apart.

Tonic eleventh chord A chord of six tones built in thirds on the first scale degree.

Tonic seventh chord A chord of four tones built in thirds on the first scale degree.

Tonicization The emphasis of a particular diatonic chord by embellishing it with an altered chord that bears a dominant relationship to it.

Traditional music Music that is based on tonal, harmonic, rhythmic, and formal practices of the so-called "common practice" period — the baroque, classical, and romantic eras.

Transient modulation Modulation to a key that is passed through quickly on the way to another key.

Treble staff The staff modified by the treble clef sign, which designates G above middle C as occurring on the second line.

Triad A chord of three tones. Most triads are built in thirds.

Triad tone A tone that is part of a triad.

Triple pedal *See also* Pedal.

Tritone Three whole steps. The interval of the augmented fourth (or diminished fifth). The tritone divides the octave into two equal parts.

U

Unessential chord A chord that is not vital to the stability of the phrase. *See also* Embellishing harmony.

Unessential dissonance Dissonance that appears incidentally, as a nonharmonic tone.

Upper voices All voices other than the lowest.

Upward stem A stem that attached to the right-hand side of the notehead and extends upward. When the grand staff is used for the four-voice chorus, soprano and tenor stems go upward.

V

Vertical aspect of harmony Chords, as opposed to chord progressions.

Voice leading The technique of moving the various voices from one chord to another.

W

Weak beat A beat that has relatively light metric stress.

Western music Music of Western Europe and music that has been derived therefrom.

Whole step The major second; two half steps.

Written root The lowest tone of a chord when arranged in thirds, as opposed to the sounding root in the case of the Italian and German sixth chords. *See* Sounding root.

Appendix D
Orchestration Chart

Note that conservative, practical ranges have been given here: In compositional assignments the extreme ranges of the instruments would probably be best avoided to facilitate classroom performances. See orchestration books in the Bibliography for information on instruments not listed here. The sounding range of the instrument is given first in wholenotes, followed by the written range in quarternotes. The transposition interval, if needed, is given just to the right of the range staff.

WOODWINDS

BRASS

* C trumpet's sounding and written range is same as Bb trumpet's written range.

+If baritone is written in treble clef, then it is written as a Bb transposition; always check with your player to see which clef should be used for your part.

STRINGS

KEYBOARD RELATED+

* *For organ (pipe or electric) or synthesizers, check with instrument/performer available to you for ranges.*

+ *Electric or synthesized piano ranges may vary from this normal piano range.*

Bibilography for Further Study

ACOUSTICS

Backus, John. *Acoustical Foundations of Music*, 2nd. ed. 1977. (ISBN 0-393-09029-9). New York: W.W. Norton.

Benade, A.H. *Fundamentals of Musical Acous - tics*. 1976. (ISBN 0-19-502030-8). Fairlawn, N.J.: Oxford University Press, Inc.

_____. *Horns, Strings & Harmony*. 1979. Reprint of 1960 ed. (ISBN 0-313-20771-2, BEHO). Westport, Conn.: Greenwood Press.

Bienvenue, Gordon F. & Prout, James H. *Acoustics for You*. 1990. Malabar, Fla.: R. E. Krieger Pub. Co.

Campbell, D.W. & Greated, Clive A. *The Musician's Guide to Acoustics*. 1987. (ISBN 0-02-870161-5). New York: Schirmer Books.

Erickson, Robert. *Sound Structure in Music*. 1975. (ISBN 0-520-02376-5). Berkeley, Calif.: University of California Press.

Moravcsik, Michael J. *Musical Sound: An Introduction to the Physics of Music*. 1987. (ISBN 0-913729-39-6). New York: Paragon House.

Pierce, John R. *The Science of Musical Sound*. 1983. (ISBN 0-7167-1508-2). New York: W.H. Freeman.

Slawson, Wayne. *Sound Color*. 1985. (ISBN 0-520-05185-8). Berkeley, Calif.: University of California Press.

COMPOSITION

Austin, Larry & Clark, Thomas. *Learning to Compose - Modes, Materials and Models of Musical Invention*. 1989. (ISBN 3495). Dubuque, Iowa: William C. Brown.

Cope, David. *New Music Composition*. 1977. (ISBN 0-02-870630-7). New York: Schirmer Books.

Dallin, Leon. *Techniques of Twentieth Century Composition: A Guide to the Materials of Modern Music*. 3rd ed. 1974. (ISBN 0-697-03614-6). Dubuque, Iowa: William C. Brown.

Hanson, Howard. *Harmonic Materials of Modern Music: Resources of the Tempered Scale*. 1960. New York: Appleton-Century-Crofts.

Marquis, G. Welton. *Twentieth-Century Music Idioms*. Reprint of 1964 ed. 1981. (ISBN 0-313-22624-5, MATC). Westport, Conn.: Greenwood Press.

Persichetti, Vincent. *Twentieth-Century Harmony: Creative Aspects and Practice*. 1961. New York: W.W. Norton.

Russo, William & Ainis, Jeffrey. *Composing Music: A New Approach*. 1983. (ISBN 0-13-164756-3). Englewood Cliffs, N.J.:Prentice-Hall.

Wourinen, Charles. *Simple Composition*. 1979. (ISBN 0-582-28059-1). New York: Longman.

COUNTERPOINT

Benjamin, Thomas. *Counterpoint in the Style of J.S. Bach*. 1986. (ISBN 0-02-870280-8). New York: Schirmer Books.

_____. *The Craft of Modal Counterpoint: A Practical Approach*. 1979. (ISBN 0-02-870480-0). New York: Schirmer Books.

Gauldin, Robert. *A Practical Approach to Sixteenth Century Counterpoint*. 1985. (ISBN 0-13-689258-2). Englewood Cliffs, N.J.: Prentice-Hall.

Kennan, Kent. *Counterpoint,* 2nd ed. 1972. (ISBN 0-13-184291-9). Englewood Cliffs, N.J.: Prentice-Hall.

Mason, Neale B. *Essentials of Eighteenth-Century Counterpoint*. 1968. (ISBN 0-697-03605-7). Dubuque, Iowa: William C. Brown.

Merriman, Margarita. *A New Look at Sixteenth-Century Counterpoint*. 1982. (ISBN 0-8191-2392-7). Lanham, Md.: University Press of America.

Parks, Richard S. *Eighteenth Century Counterpoint & Tonal Structure*. 2nd ed. 1984. (ISBN 0-13-246744-5). Englewood Cliffs, N.J.: Prentice-Hall.

Piston, Walter. *Counterpoint*. 1947. (ISBN 0-393-09728-5). New York: W.W. Norton.

Schenker, Heinrich. *Counterpoint, 2 Vols.* Rothgeb, John & Thym, Jurgen, trans. 1986. (ISBN 0-02-873220-0). New York: Schirmer Books.

Schönberg, Arnold. *Preliminary Exercises in Counterpoint*. Stein, Leonard, ed. 1982. (ISBN 0-571-09275-6). Winchester, Mass.: Faber & Faber.

Searle, Humphrey. *Twentieth-Century Counterpoint: A Guide for Students*. Reprint of 1954 ed. 1986. (ISBN 0-88355-763-0). Westport, Conn.: Hyperion Press.

Westergaard, Peter. *Introduction to Tonal Theory*. 1976. (ISBN 0-393-09342-5). New York: W.W. Norton.

EAR TRAINING/SIGHTSINGING

Blombach, Ann K. *MacGAMUT, Intervals • Scales • Chords* 1988. Mountain View, Calif.: Mayfield.

Carlsen, James C. *Melodic Perception: A Program for Self-Instruction*. 1965. (ISBN 0-07-009975-8). New York: McGraw-Hill Book Co.

Friedmann, Michael L. *Ear Training for Twentieth-Century Music*. 1990. New Haven: Yale University Press.

Gregory, David. *Melodic Dictator* (Macintosh program). 1988. Ann Arbor, Mich.: University of Michigan Center for Performing Arts and Technology.

Ghezzo, Marta A. *Solfege, Ear Training, Rhythm, Dictation & Music Theory: A Comprehensive Course.* 1980. (ISBN 0-8173-6403-X). University, Al.: University of Alabama Press.

Horacek, Leo & Lefkoff, Gerald. *Programmed Ear Training.* 4 Vols. 1970. (texts & tapes). San Diego, Calif.: Harcourt Brace Jovanovich.

Kelly, Robert. *Aural & Visual Recognition: A Musical Ear Training Series.* 1972. (ISBN 0-252-00073-0). Champaign, Ill.: University of Illinois Press.

Olson, Robert G. *Music Dictation: A Stereo Taped Series.* 1970. (ISBN 0-534-00671-X). Belmont, Calif.: Wadsworth.

Shumway, Stanley. *Harmony and Ear Training at the Keyboard.* 4th ed. 1984. Dubuque, Iowa: Wm. C. Brown.

Trubitt, Allen R. & Hines, Robert S. *Ear Training & Sight-Singing: An Integrated Approach.* 1979. (ISBN 0-02-870810-5). New York: Schirmer Books.

Wittlich, Gary & Humphries, Lee. *Ear Training: An Approach Through Music Literature.* 1974. (ISBN 0-15-518707-4). (has records, tapes or cassttes). San Diego, Calif.: Harcourt Brace Jovanovich.

Listen 2.0 (Interactive Ear Training Software for the Apple Macintosh). 1989. Menlo Park, Calif.: Resonate.

Practica Musica by ARS Nova.

Note: As this text goes to press there there continues to be a number of computer programs available and more coming out all the time.

FORM/ANALYSIS

Berry, Wallace. *Form in Music.* 2nd ed. 1986. (ISBN 0-13-329285-1). Englewood Cliffs, N.J.: Prentice-Hall.

Cook, Nicholas. *A Guide to Musical Analysis.* 1987. (ISBN 0-8076-1172-7). New York: George Braziller, Inc.

Cooper, Paul. *Perspectives in Music Theory: An Historical-Analytical Approach.* 1973. (ISBN 0-06-041368-9, HarpC). New York: Harper & Row.

Dunsby, Jonathan & Whittal, Arnold. *Musical Analysis.* 1987. (ISBN 0-300-03713-9). New Haven, Conn.: Yale University Press.

Epstein, David. *Beyond Orpheus: Studies in Musical Structure.* 1987. (ISBN 0-19-315150-2). Fairlawn, N.J.: Oxford University Press.

Forte, Allen & Gilbert, Steven E. *Introduction to Schenkerian Analysis: Form & Content in Tonal Music.* 1982. (ISBN 0-393-95192-8). New York: W.W. Norton.

Green, Douglas M. *Form in Tonal Music: An Introduction to Analysis.* 2nd ed. 1979. (ISBN 0-03-020286-8). New York: Holt, Rinehart & Winston.

Hutcheson, Jere T. *Musical Form & Analysis.* 2 Vols. (ISBN 0-8008-5454-3; 0-8008-5455-1). Boston: Taplinger.

Mason, Robert M. *Modern Methods of Music Analysis Using Computers.* 1985. (ISBN 0-9615669-0-6). Peterborough, N.H.: Schoolhouse Press.

Narmour, Eugene. *Beyond Schenkerism: The Need for Alternatives in Music Analysis.* 1980. (ISBN 0-226-56848-2, P893, Phoen). Chicago: University of Chicago Press.

Spencer, Peter & Temko, Peter M. *A Practical Approach to the Study of Form in Music.* 1988. (ISBN 0-13-689050-4). Englewood Cliffs, N.J.: Prentice-Hall.

Wade, Graham. *The Shape of Music: An Introduction to Musical Form.* 1982. (ISBN0-8052-8110-X). New York: Schocken Books, Inc.

Walton, Charles W. *Basic Forms in Music.* 1974. (ISBN 0-88284-010-X). Sherman Oaks, Calif.: Alfred Publishing.

Warfield, Gerald. *Layer Analysis: A Primer of Elementary Tonal Structures.* 1978. (ISBN 0-582-28069-9). New York: Longman.

White, John D. *The Analysis of Music.* 2nd ed. 1984. (ISBN 0-8108-1701-2). Metuchen, N.J.: Scarecrow Press.

GENERAL

Barra, Donald. *The Dynamic Performance: A Performer's Guide to Musical Expression & Interpretation.* 1983. (ISBN 13-221556-X). Englewood Cliffs, N.J.: Prentice-Hall.

Baur, John. *Music Theory Through Literature.* 2 Vols. 1985. (ISBN 0-13-607821-4; 0-13-607847-8). Englewood Cliffs, N.J.: Prentice-Hall.

Beach, David. *Aspects of Schenkerian Theory.* 1983. (ISBN 0-300-02803-2). New Haven, Conn.: Yale University Press.

Cogan, Robert. *New Images of Musical Sound.* 1984. (ISBN 0-674-61585-9). Cambridge, Mass.: Harvard University Press.

Cogan, Robert & Escot, Pozzi. *Sonic Design: The Nature of Sound & Music.* 1976. Englewood Cliffs, N.J.: Prentice-Hall.

Fotine, Larry. *Contemporary Musician's Handbook & Dictionary.* 1984. (ISBN 0-933830-03-3). Sepulveda, Calif.: Poly Tone Press.

Halloran, Mark, Ed./comp. *The Musician's Business and Legal Guide.* 1991. Englewood Cliffs, N.J.: Prentice-Hall.

Harder, Paul O. & Steinke, Greg A. *Basic Materials in Music Theory.* 7th ed. 1991. (ISBN 0-205-12999-4). Boston: Allyn and Bacon.

Harder, Paul O. & Steinke, Greg A. *Bridge To Twentieth Century Music,* 1973. (ISBN 0-205-03639-2). Boston: Allyn and Bacon, Inc. (Now published privately by Tierra del Mar Music, 1000 N. Denmark Dr., Muncie, IN 47304)

Helm, Eugene & Luper, Albert T. *Words & Music: Form & Procedure in Theses, Dissertations, Research Papers, Book Reports, Programs, & Theses in Composition.* 1971. (ISBN 0-913574-00-7). Valley Forge, Pa.: European American Music.

Hofstetter, Fred T. *Computer Literacy for Musicians.* 1988. Englewood Cliff, N.J.: Prentice-Hall.

Marin, Deborah S. & Wittlich, Gary E. *Tonal Harmony for the Keyboard: With an Introduction to Improvisation.* 1989. New: Schirmer Books.

Moore, F. Richard. *Elements of Computer Music.* 1990. Englewood Cliffs, N.J.: Prentice-Hall.

Rahn, Jay. *A Theory for All Music: Problems & Solutions in the Analysis of Non-Western Forms.* 1983. (ISBN 0-8020-5538-9). Toronto: University of Toronto Press.

Reti, Rudolph R. *The Thematic Process in Mu-sic.* Reprint of 1951 ed. 1978. (ISBN 0-8371-9875-5, RETH). Westport, Conn.: Greenwood Press, Inc.

_____. *Tonality, Atonality, Pantonality: A Study of Some Trends in Twentieth-Century Music.* Reprint of 1958 ed. 1978. (ISBN 0-313-20478-0, RETO). Westport, Conn.: Greenwood Press, Inc.

Schafer, R. Murray. *The Thinking Ear.* 1986. (C86-093409-8). Arcana Ed., PO Box 425, Sta. K., Toronto, Canada.

Simms, Bryan R. *Music of the 20th Century.* 1986 (ISBN 0-02-873020-8). New York: Schirmer Books.

Taylor, Clifford. *Musical Idea and the Design Aesthetic in Contemporary Music: a Text for Discerning Appraisal of Musical Thought in Western Culture.* 1990. Lewiston, N.Y.: Edwin Mellon Press.

Toch, Ernst. *The Shaping Forces in Music: An Inquiry into the Nature of Harmony, Melody, Counterpoint, Form.* 1977. (ISBN 0-486-23346-4). Mineola, N.Y.: Dover Publications.

MUSICAL ANTHOLOGIES

Benjamin, Thomas E. *Music for Analysis: Examples from the Common Practice Period & the Twentieth Century.* 2nd ed. 1984. (ISBN 0-395-34225-2). Boston: Houghton Mifflin.

Berry, Wallace & Chudacoff, Edward. *Eight-eenth Century Imitative Counterpoint: Music for Analysis.* 1969. (ISBN 0-13-246843-3). Englewood Cliff, N.J.: Prentice-Hall.

Bockmon, Guy A. & Starr, William J. *Scored for Listening: A Guide to Music.* 2nd ed. 1972. (ISBN 0-15-579055-2, HC) records (ISBN 0-15-579056-0). San Diego, Calif.: Harcourt Brace Jovanovich.

Brandt, William; Corra, Arthur; Christ, William; DeLeone, Richard & Winold, Allen. *The Comprehensive Study of Music.* New York: Harper & Row.

Burkhart, Charles. *Anthology for Musical Analysis.* 3rd Ed. 1979. (ISBN 0-03-018866-0). New York: Holt, Rinehart & Winston.

De Lio, Thomas & Smith, Stuart Saunders. *Twentieth Century Music Scores.* 1989. Englewood Cliffs, N.J.: Prentice-Hall.

Hardy, Gordon & Fish, Arnold. *Music Literature: A Workbook for Analysis.* 2 Vols. 1966. (ISBN 0-06-042633-0, HarpC; 0-06-042634-9). New York: Harper & Row .

Kamien, Roger, ed. *The Norton Scores: An Anthology for Listening.* 2 Vols. 4th ed. 1984. (ISBN 0-393-95304-1; 0-393-95310-6). New York: W.W. Norton.

Melcher, Robert A.; Warch, Williard F. & Mast, Paul B. *Music for Study.* 3rd ed. 1988. Englewood Cliff, N.J.: Prentice-Hall.

Palisca, Calude V., ed. *Norton Anthology of Western Music.* 2 Vols. 2nd ed. 1988. (ISBN 0-393-95642-3; 0-393-95644-X). New York: W.W. Norton.

Ward-Steinman, David & Ward-Steinman, Susan L. *Comparative Anthology of Musical Forms,* 2 Vols. Reprint of 1976 Ed. 1987. (ISBN 0-8191-5600-0). Lanham, Md: University Press of America.

Wennerstrom, Mary H. *Anthology of Musical Structure & Style.* 1983. (ISBN 0-13-038372-4). Englewood Cliff, N.J.: Prentice-Hall.

MUSICAL NOTATION

Harder, Paul O. *Music Manuscript Techniques, A Programmed Approach, 2 Parts.* 1984. (ISBN 0-205-07992-X [pt. 1], 0-205-07993-8 [pt. 2]). Boston: Allyn and Bacon, Inc.

Jarrett, Jack M. *Music Printer* (Apple IIe program) or *Music Printer Plus* (IBM program). 1987 & 1988. Bellevue, Wash.: Temporal Acuity Products, Inc.

Read, Gardner. *Music Notation.* 1979. (ISBN 0-8008-5453-5). Boston: Taplinger.

Warfield, Gerald. *How To Write Music Manuscript in Pencil.* 1977. (ISBN 0-679-30332-4). New York: Longman.

Deluxe Music Construction Set 2.5. (computer program for Macintosh), 1988. San Mateo, Calif.: Electronic Arts.

Encore. (computer program for Macintosh). 1990. Half Moon Bay, Calif.: Passport Designs.

Finale 3.0 by Coda Music Technology.

Music Prose by Coda Music Technology.

Notewriter II. (computer program for Macintosh). 1989. Half Moon Bay, Calif.: Passport Designs.

Professional Composer and *Mosaic* by Mark of the Unicorn.

Score. (computer program for IBM). 1990. Half Moon Bay, Calif.: Passport Designs.

Songworks by ARS Nova.

Note: As this text goes to press there continue to be a number of notation programs available and more coming out all the time.

ORCHESTRATION

Adler, Samuel. *The Study of Orchestration.* 1982. (ISBN 0-393-95188-X). New York: W.W. Norton.

Blatter, Alfred. *Instrumentation-Orchestration.* 1980. (ISBN 0-582-28118-0). New York: Macmillan.

Burton, Steven D. *Orchestration.* 1982. (ISBN 0-13-639500-7). Englewood Cliff, N.J.: Prentice-Hall.

Kennan, Kent & Grantham, Donald. *The Technique of Orchestration.* 3rd ed. 1983. (ISBN 0-13-900308-8). Englewood Cliff, N.J.: Prentice-Hall.

Polansky, Larry. *New Instrumentation & Orchestration: An Outline for Study.* 1986. (ISBN 0-945996-01-2). Oakland, Calif.: Frog Peak Music.

Read, Gardner. *Style & Orchestration.* 1979. (ISBN 0-02-872110-1). New York: Schirmer Books.

Stiller, Andrew. *Handbook of Instrumentation.* 1985. Berkeley, Calif.: University of California Press.

Please, again note that there are many musical computer programs based on both Apple and IBM systems appearing all the time which may relate to one or more of the above bibliographical areas. Please check with an instructor or musical computer listings for what might be currently available.

(Numbers refer to frames, except where page numbers are indicated (p. or pp.), which refer to examples used for Supplementary Assignments.)

V